EYEWITNESS
INSECT

T0286257

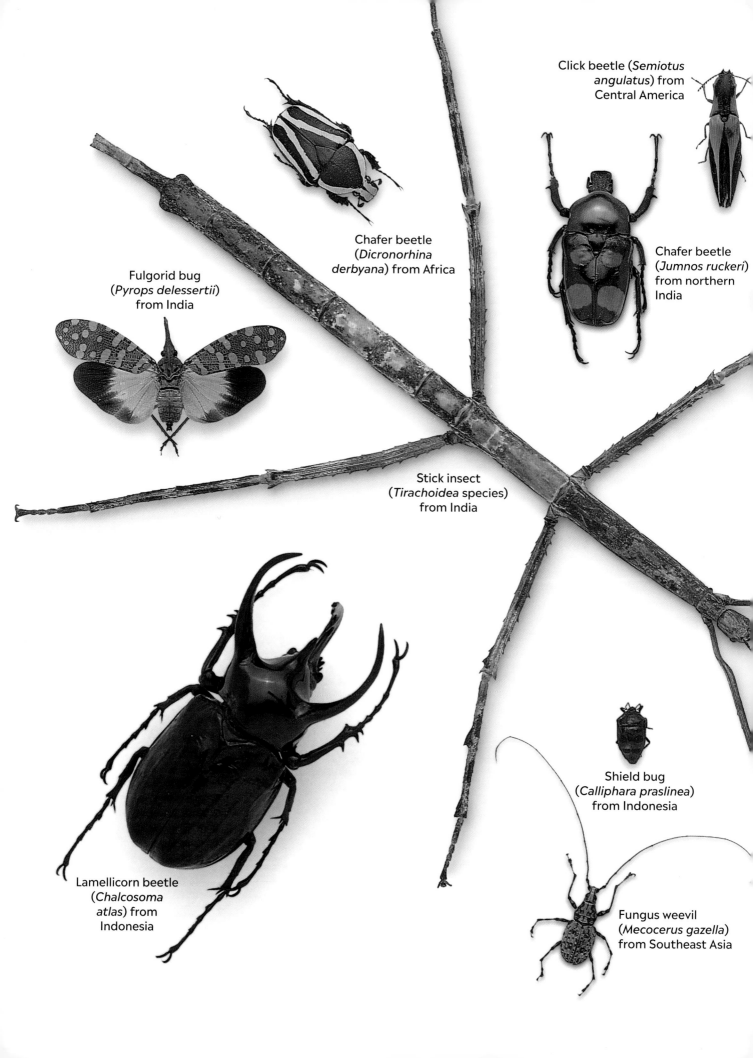

Click beetle (*Semiotus angulatus*) from Central America

Chafer beetle (*Dicronorhina derbyana*) from Africa

Chafer beetle (*Jumnos ruckeri*) from northern India

Fulgorid bug (*Pyrops delessertii*) from India

Stick insect (*Tirachoidea* species) from India

Shield bug (*Calliphara praslinea*) from Indonesia

Lamellicorn beetle (*Chalcosoma atlas*) from Indonesia

Fungus weevil (*Mecocerus gazella*) from Southeast Asia

Blowfly (*Calliphora vomitoria*) found worldwide

Tawny mining bee (*Andrena fulva*) from Europe

EYEWITNESS
INSECT

Written by

LAURENCE MOUND

Stag beetle (*Lucanus cervus*) from Europe

Bog bush-cricket (*Metrioptera brachyptera*) from Europe

Leaf beetle (*Doryphorella 22-punctata*) from South America

Tortoise beetle (*Eugenysa regalis*) from South America

Longhorn beetle (*Callipogon senex*) from Central America

Rove beetle (*Emus hirtus*) from Great Britain

Shield bug (*Sphaerocoris annulus*) from Africa

Cuckoo wasp (*Stilbum splendidum*) from Australia

Shield bug (*Cantao ocellatus*) from Indonesia

DK

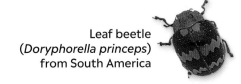

Leaf beetle (*Doryphorella princeps*) from South America

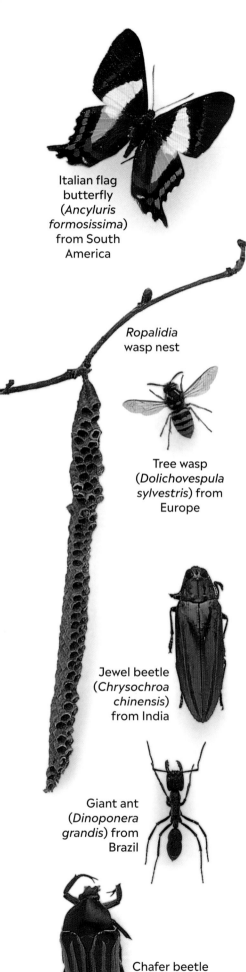

Italian flag butterfly (*Ancyluris formosissima*) from South America

Ropalidia wasp nest

Tree wasp (*Dolichovespula sylvestris*) from Europe

Jewel beetle (*Chrysochroa chinensis*) from India

Giant ant (*Dinoponera grandis*) from Brazil

Chafer beetle (*Trichaulax macleayi*) from northern Australia

DK Penguin Random House

REVISED EDITION

DK DELHI
Senior Art Editor Vikas Chauhan
Project Art Editor Heena Sharma
Editor Aashirwad Jain
Senior Managing Editor Rohan Sinha
Managing Art Editor Govind Mittal
DTP Designers Pawan Kumar, Deepak Mittal
Hi-res Coordinator Neeraj Bhatia
Jacket Designer Juhi Sheth
Senior Jackets Coordinator Priyanka Sharma Saddi
Picture Researcher Vishal Ghavri

DK LONDON
Senior Editor Carron Brown
Art Editor Chrissy Checketts
US Senior Editor Kayla Dugger
US Executive Editor Lori Cates Hand
Managing Editor Francesca Baines
Managing Art Editor Philip Letsu
Production Editor Gillian Reid
Production Controller Jack Matts
Senior Jackets Designer Surabhi Wadhwa Gandhi
Jacket Design Development Manager Sophia MTT
Publisher Andrew Macintyre
Associate Publishing Director Liz Wheeler
Art Director Karen Self
Publishing Director Jonathan Metcalf

Consultant Jon Curson

FIRST EDITION
Project Editor Helen Parker
Art Editor Peter Bailey
Senior Editor Sophie Mitchell
Senior Art Editor Julia Harris
Editorial Director Sue Unstead
Art Director Anne-Marie Bulat
Special Photography Colin Keates, Neil Fletcher, Frank Greenaway, Harold Taylor, Jane Burton, Kim Taylor, and Oxford Scientific Films

This Eyewitness ® Guide has been conceived by Dorling Kindersley Limited and Editions Gallimard

This American Edition, 2023
First American Edition, 1990
Published in the United States by DK Publishing
1745 Broadway, 20th Floor, New York, NY 10019

Copyright © 1990, 2003, 2007, 2017, 2023
Dorling Kindersley Limited
DK, a Division of Penguin Random House LLC
23 24 25 26 27 10 9 8 7 6 5 4 3 2
004–335458–Aug/2023

A catalog record for this book is available from the Library of Congress.
ISBN 978-0-7440-8156-5 (Paperback)
ISBN 978-0-7440-8157-2 (ALB)

DK books are available at special discounts when purchased in bulk for sales promotions, premiums, fund-raising, or educational use. For details, contact:
DK Publishing Special Markets,
1745 Broadway, 20th Floor, New York, NY 10019
SpecialSales@dk.com

Printed and bound in China

For the curious
www.dk.com

MIX
Paper | Supporting responsible forestry
FSC™ C018179

This book was made with Forest Stewardship Council™ certified paper—one small step in DK's commitment to a sustainable future.
For more information go to www.dk.com/our-green-pledge

Dung beetle (*Coprophanaeus lancifer*) from South America

Longhorn beetle (*Sternotomis bohemani*) from East Africa

Tiger beetle (*Manticora scabra*) from East Africa

Golden-ringed dragonfly (*Cordulegaster boltonii*) from the UK

Contents

Lamellicorn larva
(*Oryctes centaurus*)
from New Guinea

The parts of an insect

Once an insect has reached adult size, it never grows any larger. This is because its entire body is covered by a hard external skeleton made of a horny substance called chitin. Young insects shed, or molt, this "exoskeleton" several times before they become adults. The insect takes in extra air to make itself larger and splits the old skin, which falls off to reveal the new skeleton beneath.

An **insect body** is divided into **three parts**: the head, thorax, and abdomen.

Claw

Tarsus

Tibia

Femur

Folding point

Front, or leading edge of wing

Tip, or apex, of wing

Base of wing folds underneath

Hind wing folded

In order to fit beneath the wing cases, the hind wings must be folded. The wing tip folds back at a special break called the folding point. The base of the wing is also folded underneath.

Abdomen

The abdomen, containing the digestive system, heart, and reproductive organs, is protected by the rigid exoskeleton, or cuticle. But between the segments, the body is flexible. The whole surface is covered by a thin layer of wax, which helps prevent water loss.

Beetle body

This jewel beetle (*Euchroma gigantea*) from South America is a typical insect with jointed legs and three distinct body regions: the head, thorax (chest), and abdomen. These regions are made up of ringlike segments.

Front wings

In beetles, the front pair of wings is adapted as a pair of hard wing cases called elytra. These protect the body and are often brightly colored.

INTERNAL ANATOMY

This diagram shows a worker bee's internal anatomy. The digestive system (yellow) is a long tube divided into the foregut, midgut, and hindgut. The respiratory system (white) contains a network of tubes through which air passes from the spiracles to other body parts. In the abdomen, two large air sacs supply air to the flight muscles in the thorax. The nervous system (blue) is formed by one main nerve, which has knots of nerve cells, or ganglia, along its length. The ganglion in the head is the bee's brain.

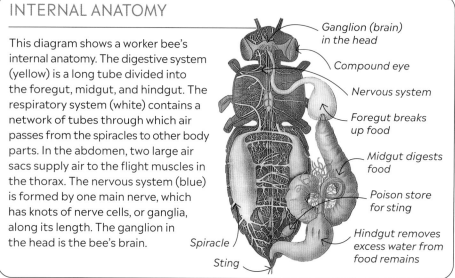

Ganglion (brain) in the head

Compound eye

Nervous system

Foregut breaks up food

Midgut digests food

Poison store for sting

Hindgut removes excess water from food remains

Spiracle

Sting

Legs

Insects have three pairs of jointed legs made up of four main parts: the coxa joins the leg to the thorax; the femur (thigh) is the most muscular section of the leg; the tibia (lower leg) often carries spines for self-defense; and the tarsus (foot) has two claws that often contain a small pad for gripping onto smooth surfaces.

Tarsus has between one and five segments

Tibia

Femur

Coxa

Coxa

Thorax

The thorax is made up of three segments. The first bears the first pair of legs, while the second and third segments each bear a pair of wings and a pair of legs.

Each foot bears two claws for climbing on rough surfaces.

Feeding in information

The head houses the brain and important sense organs such as the eyes, the antennae, and the palps (feelers), which give the insect information about the taste and smell of its food.

Segmented antenna detects vibrations and smells

Compound eyes

"Compound" eyes consist of hundreds of tiny, simple eyes, which can detect movement in almost every direction at once.

Compound eye

First segment of thorax bears front legs

Antennae

Antennae can be long and thin, as in crickets, or short and hairlike, as in some flies. But whatever their shape, they bear many sensory structures that are able to detect smells and air movements.

Claw

Second and third segments of the thorax

Leading edge of hind wing

Hind wing outstretched

As the wing cases are lifted, muscles inside the thorax pull on the leading edge of the hind wings, making them open.

Wing case, or elytron

A breath of fresh air

Insects, including this puss moth caterpillar, breathe air through a network of tubes (tracheae) that extend into the body from pairs of openings in the cuticle called spiracles.

What is an **insect?**

Insects are the most successful creatures in the animal kingdom. They are found in all types of habitats, both on land and in water. Their size means they can fit into very small places and need little food to live. Insects are arthropods—a type of invertebrate (animal without a backbone). They have a hard, protective exoskeleton and jointed legs. However, insects are different from other arthropods because they have only six legs. Each species is a member of a larger group, or order, made up of other insects with similar physical features.

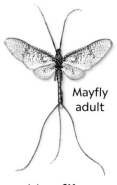

Mayflies

Mayflies belong to the order Ephemeroptera. The adults often live no longer than a day.

Mayfly adult

Flies

Fly

Flies belong to the order called Diptera, meaning "two wings," because, unlike other insects, flies have only one pair of wings.

Ground beetle

Wasp

Bee

Ant

Ladybug beetle

Beetles

Beetles belong to the order Coleoptera. They have tough front wings (elytra) that fold over the hind wings and body like a protective case.

Cockroaches

Cockroaches belong to the order Blattodea, which also includes termites. Adult cockroaches have hardened front wings that overlap each other. Young cockroaches are wingless.

Piercing, sucking mouthparts

Stick insect

Bug

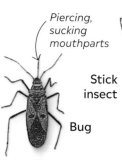

Wasps, ants, and bees

These insects belong to the order Hymenoptera and have two pairs of thin, veined wings. Many females in this group, and workers of social species (see pp.38–39), are armed with a sting.

Bugs

True bugs belong to the order Hemiptera, which means "half wing." The front wings of many larger bugs have hard bases with soft tips.

Earwig

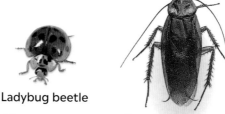

Dragonfly

Butterfly

Dragonflies and damselflies

These closely related insects belong to the order Odonata. Their large jaws are specially adapted to catch flies.

Earwigs

Earwigs belong to the order Dermaptera. Their hind wings are folded under their very short front wings.

Stick insects

These insects belong to the order Phasmatodea. When resting, they look just like the leaves and twigs they eat.

Butterflies and moths

Butterflies and moths belong to the order Lepidoptera. The tiny scales on their wings give them their beautiful colors.

Moth

Crickets and grasshoppers

These insects have strong hind legs used for jumping and singing. They belong to the order Orthoptera.

Grasshopper

Not insects

Many people confuse other arthropods with insects. Spiders and scorpions have four pairs of legs rather than three, as in insects, but their head and thorax are fused together. Unlike insects, they have no wings and no antennae. Crabs, prawns, woodlice, and centipedes all have many more jointed legs than insects. In contrast, an earthworm has no legs at all. Slugs, snails, and starfish have a very different structure that is not based on segments.

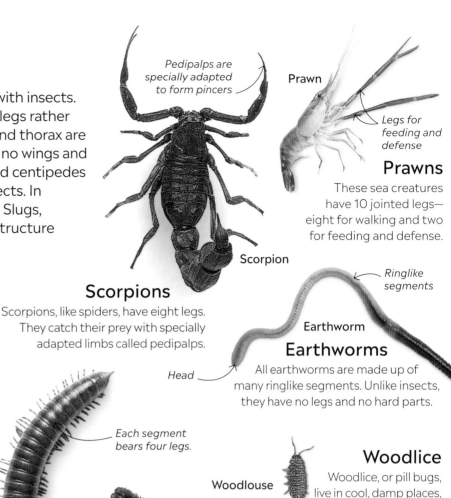

Pedipalps are specially adapted to form pincers

Prawn

Legs for feeding and defense

Prawns

These sea creatures have 10 jointed legs—eight for walking and two for feeding and defense.

Scorpion

Scorpions

Scorpions, like spiders, have eight legs. They catch their prey with specially adapted limbs called pedipalps.

Ringlike segments

Earthworm

Earthworms

All earthworms are made up of many ringlike segments. Unlike insects, they have no legs and no hard parts.

Head

Beach fleas

These strange creatures look like insects, but they have 10 legs rather than six. They live in damp sand on beaches all over the world.

Each segment bears four legs.

Millipede

Millipedes

It is easy to see a millipede's head because, like insects, it has a pair of antennae. Its body is divided into many segments, each of which bears two pairs of legs.

Antenna

Woodlice

Woodlouse

Woodlice, or pill bugs, live in cool, damp places, under stones and logs. When danger threatens, they roll into a tight, round ball of scaly armor.

Leg

Chelicerae (jaws)

Pedipalps used as feelers

Tarantula

"Poison claws"— modified front legs—are used to catch prey

Centipedes

Unlike millipedes, centipedes have only one pair of legs on each segment. They capture their prey with their "poison claws," specially adapted front pair of legs with fangs. Large species can give a painful bite.

Centipede

Spiders

This tarantula from Sri Lanka is one of the world's largest spiders. The leglike pedipalps next to the head are used as feelers. The large jaws inject poison into their prey and, as in all spiders, the food is sucked into the body as a liquid.

The first insects

The first winged insects appeared on Earth more than 300 million years ago. Early fossils show that a few of these insects, such as dragonflies and cockroaches, would have looked very similar to present-day species. But most of the oldest insect fossils represent groups that are no longer alive today. Some of these early insects were probably hindered by large, unfolding wings, with spans of up to 30 in (70 cm), that prevented them from making a quick escape and made them sitting targets for hungry predators.

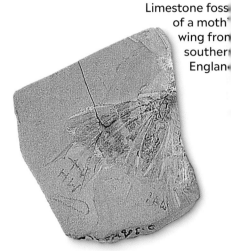

Limestone fossil of a moth's wing from southern England

Show your colors
Pigments in the scales of this fossilized wing have altered the process of fossilization so that parts of the pattern can still be seen.

 EYEWITNESS

Discovering ancient insects
George Poinar Jr. is an American entomologist and writer who studies fossilized insects in amber. His discoveries include the oldest-known bee and the first-known bat fly fossils. His idea of extracting DNA from insects fossilized in amber was adapted by American author Michael Crichton for the science-fiction novel and film *Jurassic Park*.

How amber is formed

Amber is the fossil resin of pine trees that grew over 40 million years ago. Insects attracted by the sweet scent became trapped on its sticky surface. In time, the resin, including the trapped insects, hardened and was buried in the soil. Millions of years later, it was then washed into the sea.

Bee in copal
This magnified piece of copal (a type of resin) shows a beautifully preserved "sweat bee." The bee looks very like the present-day specimen (below right).

Wing

Delicate legs

Crane fly

Modern-day "sweat bee" (*Trigona* species)

Crawling and flying insects are trapped forever in the resin released by tree trunks.

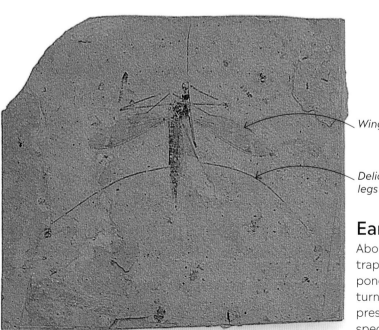

Early cranes
About 35 million years ago, this crane fly (left) became trapped in muddy sediment at the bottom of a lake or pond in the US. The sediment was so fine that when it turned to stone, even details of the wings and legs were preserved. With its floppy legs and wings, this fossilized specimen looks very similar to modern crane flies.

Oldest dragonfly

This fossilized folded wing, found in England, belongs to the oldest-known dragonfly. The dragonfly flew 300 million years ago and had a total wingspan of 8 in (20 cm), much larger than that of modern species.

Broken wing

Flowering plants

The arrival of flowering plants about 100 million years ago created a new source of food for insects in the form of pollen and nectar. Insects thrived because of this new food, and the flowering plants thrived because of the variety of pollinating insects.

Largest dragonfly

Tetracanthagyna plagiata (right) from Borneo is a member of the largest dragonfly species still in existence, with a wingspan of 6 in (15 cm). The largest dragonfly ever known is a fossilized specimen from the US, with a wingspan of 24 in (60 cm).

Compound eye

Veins

Abdomen

Unlike the wings of more recently developed insects, dragonfly wings do not fold back along the body.

Black spot, or stigma

Tip of abdomen

Veins on wings

Dragonfly predators

The artist of this engraving (above) clearly had more imagination than biological knowledge. Fossils prove that early dragonflies were skilled fliers and would not have been so easily caught by a pterosaur.

Pair of pincers, called forceps

Drowned earwig

The lake deposits at Florissant, Colorado, are about 35 million years old. They contain many well-preserved insect fossils because of the fine sediment from which the rocks were formed.

Present-day earwig (*Labidura riparia*)

Turned to stone

Even though this fossilized dragonfly appears to be missing a wing, the veins on the other wings can be seen quite clearly.

Wings and **flight**

Insects were the first creatures to fly. Flight enabled them to search for food and to escape quickly from predators. Later, wings became important for attracting a mate—by being brightly colored, by producing a scent, or by making sounds. The first flying insects had two pairs of wings that did not fold. More recent insects, such as wasps, butterflies, and beetles, have developed various mechanisms for linking their front and hind wings to produce two rather than four flight surfaces that beat together. The true flies have lost one pair of wings altogether.

Crumpled wings

A newly emerged adult cicada has soft, crumpled wings. Blood pumps into the wings' veins, making them expand. As the veins harden, the wings straighten, ready for flight.

Cricket songs

Male crickets produce "songs" with their wings to attract mates. The base of the left front wing (far left) has a rigid file that is scraped against a drumlike area on the right front wing (left).

Fringed wings

Small insects often have difficulty flying. The fringed veins on this magnified mosquito wing probably act like the flaps on an airplane wing, helping reduce "drag."

Fringed veins

Mosquito wing

1 Before takeoff

Like any airplane, a large insect such as this cockchafer beetle (*Melolontha melolontha*) must warm up its engines before flying. Before taking to the air, beetles will often open and shut their wing cases several times to check that they are in good working order. It is not unusual to see moths rapidly vibrating their wings before takeoff to warm up their flight muscles.

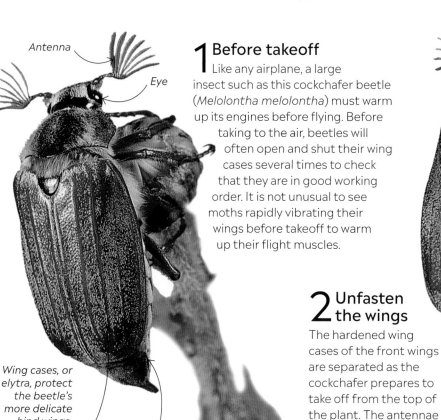

Antenna

Eye

Wing cases, or elytra, protect the beetle's more delicate hind wings, which are folded up underneath.

Abdomen

Antenna spread to sense the air currents

Claws on feet enable beetle to grip plant firmly, ready for takeoff

Large hind wings unfold

Wing cases start to open

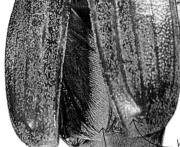

Hind wings folded beneath wing cases

2 Unfasten the wings

The hardened wing cases of the front wings are separated as the cockchafer prepares to take off from the top of the plant. The antennae are spread to check the air currents.

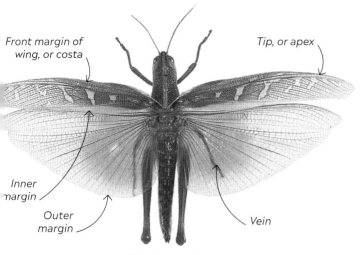

Front margin of wing, or costa

Tip, or apex

Inner margin

Outer margin

Vein

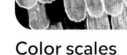

Color scales

The overlapping scales on butterfly wings are really flattened, ridged hairs that often form beautiful patterns.

Flash colors

Many insects that are perfectly camouflaged when at rest have brightly colored wings, which they flash when disturbed. As soon as the insect settles again, it seems to disappear, thus confusing the predator. This grasshopper (*Ornithacris pictula magnifica*) probably uses its lilac wings for this purpose.

Balancing

Insects often have great difficulty balancing in gusty winds. Flies have overcome such problems by reducing one pair of wings to special knoblike balancing organs, called halteres; these are probably important for landing upside-down on ceilings.

Halteres help fly balance in the air

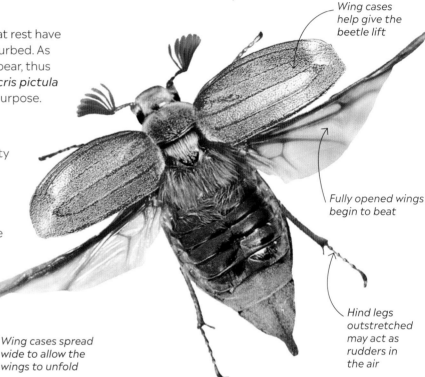

Wing cases help give the beetle lift

Fully opened wings begin to beat

Hind legs outstretched may act as rudders in the air

4 We have liftoff

With a spring from the legs, the cockchafer rises upward. The hind wings provide the driving force, but the curve of the rigid front wings provides lift as the speed increases.

Wing cases spread wide to allow the wings to unfold

Joint in wing unfolds

3 Reach for the sky

The wing cases are spread, and the thin membranous hind wings, which provide the driving force, automatically unfold as they are raised. In this vulnerable position, the beetle cannot afford to hesitate.

Wing membrane

Segmented abdomen

MOVING THE WINGS

Most of the power for flapping the wings is provided by large horizontal and vertical muscles in the thorax. Other muscles at the base of the wings adjust the angle of each stroke and determine the direction of flight.

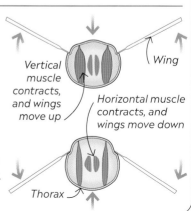

Vertical muscle contracts, and wings move up

Wing

Horizontal muscle contracts, and wings move down

Thorax

Through an insect's eyes

We do not know what sort of image insects have of the world. We know that a bee can see a person move several yards away—but does it just see a moving shape, or can it tell that the shape is a human? We also know that some bugs are attracted to ultraviolet light and the color yellow but are not attracted to blue or red. But do they see colors or shades of black and white? Dragonflies can catch mosquitoes in flight at dusk, when it is dark—does the dragonfly see them, or does it respond to their sound and movement? The subject of insect senses is full of such questions.

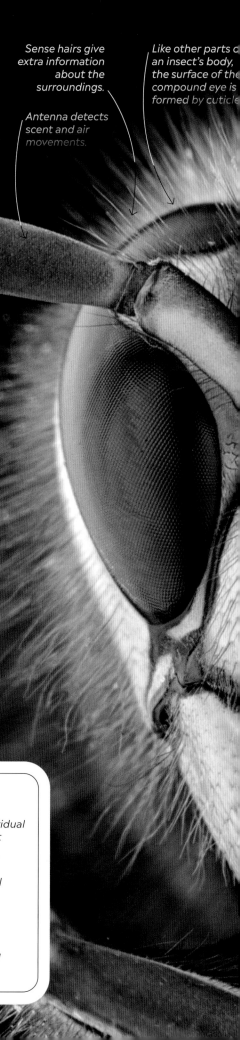

Sense hairs give extra information about the surroundings.

Antenna detects scent and air movements.

Like other parts of an insect's body, the surface of the compound eye is formed by cuticle.

Natural light   **Ultraviolet light**

Ultraviolet light

These two brimstone butterflies have been photographed in natural light (left) and in ultraviolet light (right). Insects may not see a yellow butterfly with four orange spots, but a gray insect with two large dark gray areas. Many flowers rely on ultraviolet vision to attract pollinating bees; the bees are guided to the nectar by lines called honey guides, which are visible only in ultraviolet light.

Inside an insect's eye

Insects and some other arthropods, such as crustaceans, have compound eyes. Each compound eye is made up of hundreds of facets, or ommatidia. Each facet is a mini-eye, consisting of a lens at the surface with a second corneal lens inside. These focus the light down a structure called the rhabdom, which connects to the optic nerve and brain.

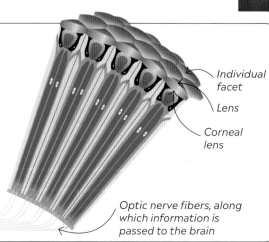

Individual facet

Lens

Corneal lens

Optic nerve fibers, along which information is passed to the brain

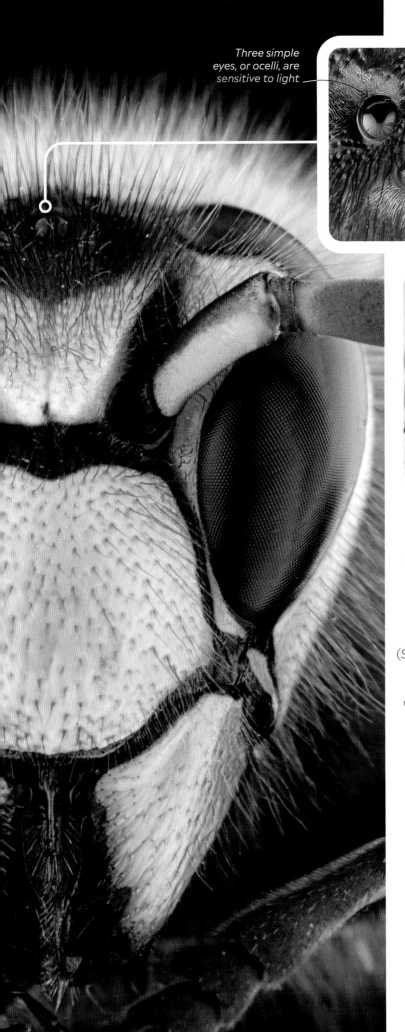

Three simple eyes, or ocelli, are sensitive to light

A waspish face

A typical insect has a pair of large compound eyes as well as three simple eyes on top. The compound eyes of this European hornet (*Vespa crabro*) extend low down on the cheeks toward the jaws. They enable insects to detect fast movements and see in a wide angle all around their body, helping them spot prey and predators.

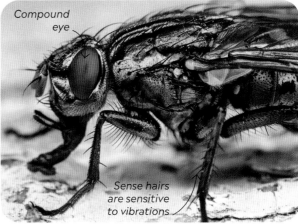

Compound eye

Sense hairs are sensitive to vibrations

Fleshfly

The hundreds of individual eye facets glow red in this fleshfly's head (right). We do not know exactly what it sees, but we do know that it can detect even the tiniest movements, making it very difficult to catch.

Black fly eyes

The head of this black fly (*Simulium* species) has been highly magnified to show the large, many-faceted compound eyes extending around the bases of the antennae. The surface of each of its tiny eyes is covered in tiny ridges and peglike tubercles.

I'm watching you

The individual eyes, or facets, that form a mantis's compound eye are very small, allowing it to respond quickly to tiny movements. It often nods and tilts its head from side to side as it sizes up potential prey and estimates the distance for its attack.

Touch, smell, and **hearing**

For many insects, the world is probably a pattern of smells and tastes. Alarm chemicals are produced by many insects so that the other members of a colony can respond quickly. Ants lay down a chemical trail and constantly touch each other to pass on their nest odor. Female moths produce chemicals capable of attracting males from great distances. Insects can also detect vibrations and sounds undetected by humans either through well-formed "ears," as on the front legs of crickets and on the abdomen of grasshoppers, or through the legs and antennae.

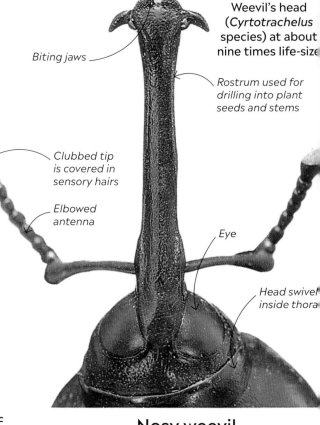

Weevil's head (*Cyrtotrachelus* species) at about nine times life-size

Biting jaws

Rostrum used for drilling into plant seeds and stems

Clubbed tip is covered in sensory hairs

Elbowed antenna

Eye

Head swivels inside thorax

Nosy weevil
The biting jaws of a weevil are at the end of the long snout, or rostrum. The sensory hairs on the tips of the "elbowed" antennae are used to explore the surface the weevil is feeding on.

Magnified hairs
These hairs (left) from around the mouth of a carpet beetle larva have been magnified 1,000 times. Each hair has its own "ball and socket" joint at the base and ridged sides. The hairs are probably used for detecting vibrations.

Antenna
The surface of this butterfly antenna is covered with tiny sensitive pegs, or tubercles, and there are thin areas of cuticle with minute scent-sensitive hairs.

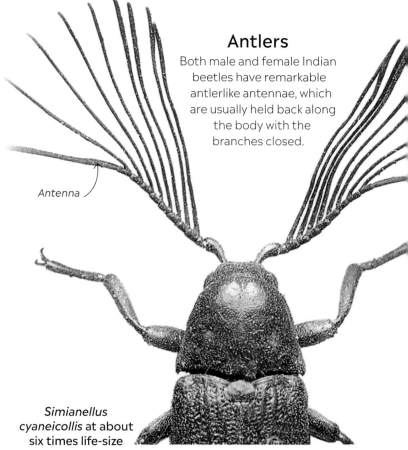

Antlers
Both male and female Indian beetles have remarkable antlerlike antennae, which are usually held back along the body with the branches closed.

Antenna

Simianellus cyaneicollis at about six times life-size

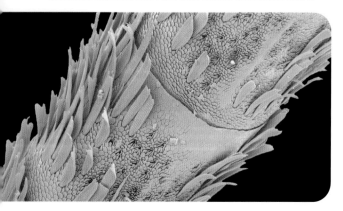

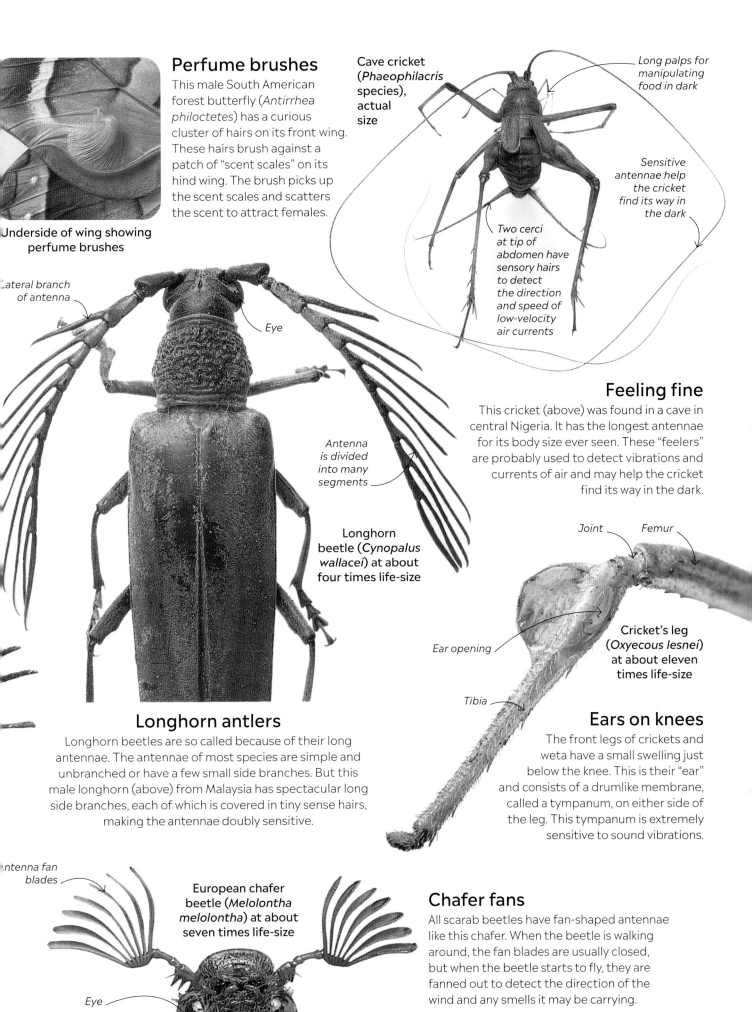

Perfume brushes

This male South American forest butterfly (*Antirrhea philoctetes*) has a curious cluster of hairs on its front wing. These hairs brush against a patch of "scent scales" on its hind wing. The brush picks up the scent scales and scatters the scent to attract females.

Underside of wing showing perfume brushes

Cave cricket (*Phaeophilacris* species), actual size

Long palps for manipulating food in dark

Sensitive antennae help the cricket find its way in the dark

Two cerci at tip of abdomen have sensory hairs to detect the direction and speed of low-velocity air currents

Lateral branch of antenna

Eye

Antenna is divided into many segments

Longhorn beetle (*Cynopalus wallacei*) at about four times life-size

Feeling fine

This cricket (above) was found in a cave in central Nigeria. It has the longest antennae for its body size ever seen. These "feelers" are probably used to detect vibrations and currents of air and may help the cricket find its way in the dark.

Joint

Femur

Ear opening

Cricket's leg (*Oxyecous lesnei*) at about eleven times life-size

Tibia

Longhorn antlers

Longhorn beetles are so called because of their long antennae. The antennae of most species are simple and unbranched or have a few small side branches. But this male longhorn (above) from Malaysia has spectacular long side branches, each of which is covered in tiny sense hairs, making the antennae doubly sensitive.

Ears on knees

The front legs of crickets and weta have a small swelling just below the knee. This is their "ear" and consists of a drumlike membrane, called a tympanum, on either side of the leg. This tympanum is extremely sensitive to sound vibrations.

Antenna fan blades

European chafer beetle (*Melolontha melolontha*) at about seven times life-size

Eye

Chafer fans

All scarab beetles have fan-shaped antennae like this chafer. When the beetle is walking around, the fan blades are usually closed, but when the beetle starts to fly, they are fanned out to detect the direction of the wind and any smells it may be carrying.

17

Legwork

Legs are important to most animals for walking, running, and jumping, as well as for keeping the body off the ground. Insects have found even more uses for their legs. Bees have little brushes and baskets on their legs for collecting and storing pollen. Many insects' legs are modified for fighting or for holding onto the opposite sex when mating. Some water insects have flattened legs with long hairs that work like oars; others have long, delicate, stiltlike legs for walking on the surface without sinking.

Cleaning legs

Flies are covered in hairs, which they clean regularly by rubbing their legs on different body parts. This helps them fly effectively. The feet of houseflies have special pads between the claws that enable them to walk upside-down on smooth surfaces.

Propellerlike feet can bury this cricket in seconds

Wings coiled lik[e] a spring

Going dow[n]

The propellerlike feet o[f] this desert-dwelling cricke[t] enable it to dig a hole i[n] the sand and disappear i[n] seconds. The ends of th[e] wings are coiled to kee[p] them out of the wa[y]

Hind wings tilted above body

2 Preparing to jump

The locust gets ready to jump by bringing its hind legs into its body. The large muscles in the femur (thigh) are attached to the tip of the tibia (shinbone). When these muscles shorten, or contrac[t] the leg straightens, throwing the insect into the air.

Front legs outstretched, ready for touchdown

Femur *Compound eye*

Tibia

Front wings curved to scoop up the air

1 Touching down

Landing safely is always a problem when flying. This locust has its legs spread wide, its hind wings tilted, and its front wings curved to catch the maximum amount of air. The wing shape of birds is adjusted in the same way when landing, to enable them to slow down and drop gently to the ground.

Mottled markings on wings help conceal insect on the ground

A tiny flea can jump up to 12 in (30 cm) into the air, which is the same as a person jumping 25 ft (7.5 m) off the ground.

Pseudofeet

The "legs" on the abdomen of caterpillars, known as prolegs, are actually muscular extensions of the body wall. Caterpillars use these prolegs for movement.

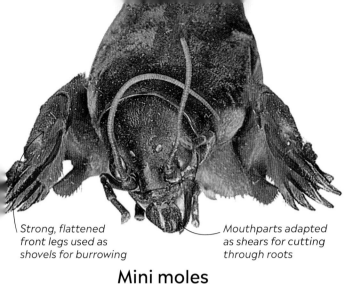

Strong, flattened front legs used as shovels for burrowing

Mouthparts adapted as shears for cutting through roots

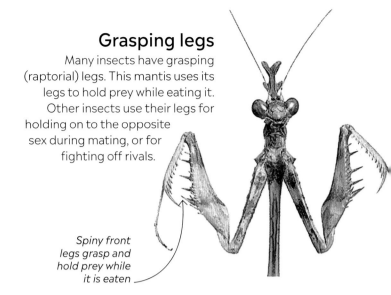

Grasping legs

Many insects have grasping (raptorial) legs. This mantis uses its legs to hold prey while eating it. Other insects use their legs for holding on to the opposite sex during mating, or for fighting off rivals.

Spiny front legs grasp and hold prey while it is eaten

Mini moles

Mole crickets (*Gryllotalpa gryllotalpa,* above), like moles, have unusually strong and flattened front legs that serve as shovels for burrowing into the soil. As they tunnel underground, they eat roots, which they cut through with pecially adapted mouthparts that work like a pair of shears. When very active, they may become pests of grass lawns.

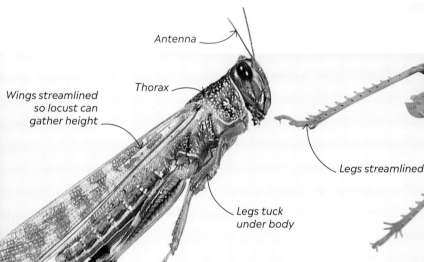

Antenna

Thorax

Wings streamlined so locust can gather height

Legs tuck under body

Front and hind wings open wide

Legs streamlined

3 Gathering height

In order to get as high as possible, the locust makes its body streamlined. The wings remain closed, and the legs are tucked under. Although small, the leg muscles of locusts are extremely powerful. The longest jump by a locust is about 20 in (50 cm), which is equal to 10 times its body length.

4 Midleap

Once the locust has gotten as high as it can, it opens both pairs of wings wide and flaps them rapidly. The hind legs are still streamlined, but the front legs move forward as the locust prepares to land again.

Moles

Although moles are totally unrelated to mole crickets (above), which are insects, they have similarly adapted, shovel-like front legs for burrowing in soil.

Hiding behind your own legs

The color and shape of the extensions on the legs of this leaf insect break up the outline of the legs. This helps protect the insect from predators.

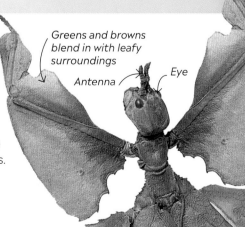

Greens and browns blend in with leafy surroundings

Antenna

Eye

Mouthparts and **feeding**

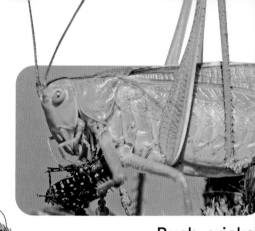

Most insects have three pairs of jaws. The mandibles are used for chewing, while the maxillae help push food into the mouth. The third pair forms the lower lip (labium). In some insects, the jaws are modified into piercing needles, long sucking tubes, or absorbent sponges.

Compound eye

Bush-cricke

This great green bush-cricke is feeding on a beetle. It hold the insect with its front leg while the large and powerf sawlike mandibles chew it u

Fly head

In houseflies and blowflies, the mandible and maxillae are not developed. The spongelike structure used by these flies to pick up liquids is formed from the labium which is simply the lower lip in other insects.

Spongelike labium for absorbing liquids

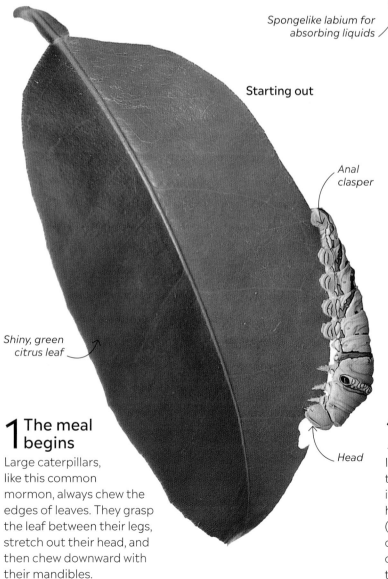

Starting out

After two hours

Anal clasper

Head

Shiny, green citrus leaf

Head

Tru legs

Proleg

Anal claspe

1 The meal begins

Large caterpillars, like this common mormon, always chew the edges of leaves. They grasp the leaf between their legs, stretch out their head, and then chew downward with their mandibles.

2 Steady progress

In addition to the three pairs of legs on its thorax, a caterpillar has four pairs of prolegs (see p.18) on the abdomen and a pair of anal claspers. Like other insects, caterpillars have an exoskeleton that they molt as they grow.

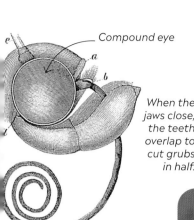

Compound eye

When the jaws close, the teeth overlap to cut grubs in half.

Butterfly head

This engraving shows how a butterfly's feeding tube (proboscis) coils up under the head. Adult butterflies do not have mandibles. The proboscis is made from the maxillae, each of which has become very long and pressed against the other.

All cut up

The teeth on the jaws of this East African ground beetle overlap when the jaws close. This scissorlike action enables it to cut up grubs and even large beetles in the soil.

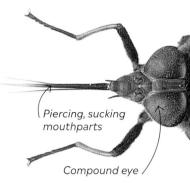

Piercing, sucking mouthparts

Compound eye

Piercing mouthparts

This tabanid fly has long mouthparts for drinking nectar from flowers. Many types of tabanid flies use their mouthparts to pierce the skin and suck up blood. They can feed on humans, but they usually feed on the blood of monkeys. These flies are not delicate feeders like mosquitoes and produce a very painful open wound.

Ants and aphids

Ants often protect small plant-sucking bugs, such as aphids, by making a shelter over them. They feed on "honeydew," a sugary substance produced by the aphids that would otherwise build up and kill the aphid colony. One way to control aphid populations on trees is to stop the ants from climbing up and protecting them.

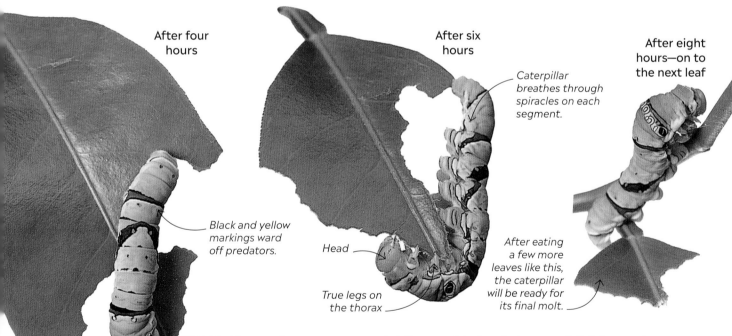

After four hours

After six hours

After eight hours—on to the next leaf

Caterpillar breathes through spiracles on each segment.

Black and yellow markings ward off predators.

Head

True legs on the thorax

After eating a few more leaves like this, the caterpillar will be ready for its final molt.

3 Halfway there
The caterpillar works its way up and down the leaf.

4 The end is in sight
Caterpillars usually feed at night to avoid predators.

5 Dinner is over
After eight hours, the leaf has gone, and the caterpillar is ready to look for the next one.

Indian moon moth larva

Chewing away on leaves, the Indian moon moth caterpillar is very exposed to predators. The spiny tubercles on its back will deter some birds from eating such a spiky morsel.

Into battle

Some species of insects, such as grasshoppers and cockroaches, produce very large numbers of offspring, but limited supplies of plants to feed them, as well as hungry predators, help limit insect populations. Some insects, such as those beetles that feed on dead wood, compete for both food and breeding sites. The males of many of these beetle species have large horns or jaws to fight off rivals.

Jaws encircle rival beetle

Digging deep

Grasshoppers lay their eggs around grass roots. In contrast, locusts and also this great green bush-cricket (*Tettigonia viridissima*) drill into the soil with a long, straight ovipositor and lay their eggs underground. They then fill in the hole and rake over the surface to conceal it from parasites.

Eggs are laid underground with the help of the ovipositor.

Males in many animal species fight to **prove dominance** and **defend territory**.

Hard wing case, or elytron, protects more delicate hind wings and abdomen underneath

Segmented tarsus

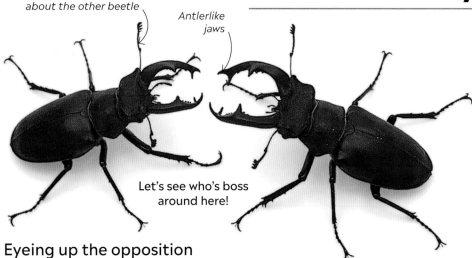

Antenna outstretched—possibly to pick up information about the other beetle

Antlerlike jaws

Let's see who's boss around here!

2 The fight
When threats are not enough, the defending male will grapple with its rival, and each beetle will attempt to lift the other off its feet by grasping it around the middl with its horns. Once this is done, it is a simple matter to throw the rival onto the ground.

Claws on tarsus help beetle take a firm grip on the ground it is defending

1 Eyeing up the opposition
Stag beetles, like these two from Europe (*Lucanus cervus*), get their name from the large branched "horns" of the male. These are really greatly enlarged jaws that are used for fighting, much like a real stag uses his antlers. A male defends his territory, usually at dusk, by adopting a threatening position.

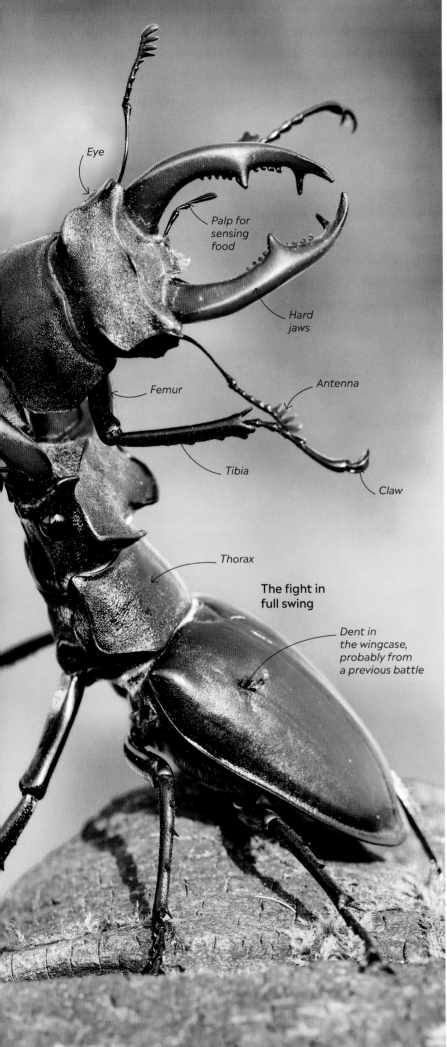

Eye

Palp for sensing food

Hard jaws

Femur

Antenna

Tibia

Claw

Thorax

The fight in full swing

Dent in the wingcase, probably from a previous battle

Antenna

Very small jaws or "horns"

Female stag beetle

No horns

Female stag beetles do not have large fighting jaws. This is because the females are not concerned with defending feeding and breeding sites. Curiously, very small male stag beetles also do not have large fighting jaws. It seems that small males are successful at times when there is not enough food to produce large males.

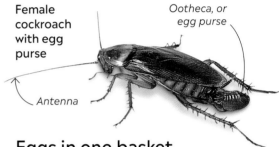

Female cockroach with egg purse

Ootheca, or egg purse

Antenna

Eggs in one basket

Cockroaches lay their eggs in groups, like grasshoppers. But whereas the egg pods of grasshoppers are made of soil, a female cockroach produces a hard, purselike structure called an ootheca, with two rows of eggs standing upright inside.

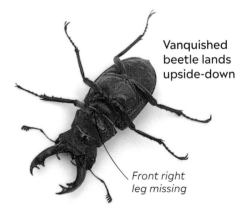

Vanquished beetle lands upside-down

Front right leg missing

3 Vanquished

If the defeated beetle lands on its back, it may be unable to get to its feet before being eaten by ants—particularly if, like this one, it has been injured. Sometimes, the teeth on the encircling jaws of the winner may punch a hole in the rival's armor, and this will be enough to kill it.

Complete
metamorphosis

Metamorphosis means "change of body form and appearance." The most advanced insects go through several stages of growth before turning into adults, in a process known as complete metamorphosis. The eggs hatch to produce larvae (caterpillars, grubs, or maggots) that are quite unlike adult insects. The larvae grow and molt several times, finally producing a pupa (chrysalis). Inside the pupa, the whole body is reorganized, and a winged adult then emerges.

Mating
Male and female Mexican bean beetles look very similar and mate frequently.

Eggs
Female Mexican bean beetles lay their eggs in large groups on the underside of leaves. Each egg stands on end and takes about a week to hatch.

Larva emerges.

Cap

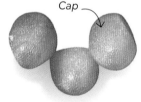

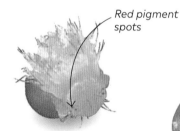

Red pigment spots

1 Egg hatches
Pores at the top of the egg allow air to reach the larva inside. About a week after the egg has been laid, the cap at the top breaks and the larva emerges.

2 Larva emerges
Three red pigment spots can be seen on either side of the larva's head. These spots are associated with simple eyes.

3 A first meal
As soon as the larva emerges from the egg, it turns around and eats the shell, which contains valuable nutrients.

4 About to change
The larva attaches itself to the underside of a leaf, ready to pupate. The larval skin is shed, revealing soft, new pupal skin, which hardens quickly.

Eggs

Young larva

Mature larva

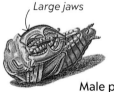

Large jaws

Male pupa

Female pupa

Stag beetles
The larvae of stag beetles always adopt a C-shaped posture. The male pupa can be distinguished from the female by its large jaws.

Scorpion flies
This drawing shows a scorpion fly larva and a pupa with well-developed wing buds.

Wing bud

Pupa

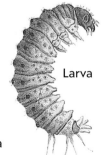

Larva

Larva feeding on plant shoot

Eating leaves

Mexican bean beetles feed on the fleshy parts of leaves both as larvae and adults.

A man transformed

In Franz Kafka's novel *Metamorphosis*, a man is transformed into an insect.

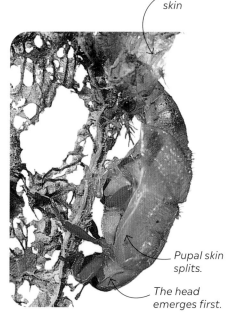

Old larval skin with long spines

Dead, lacy leaves on which larvae have fed

New pupal skin with short spines

Larval skin

Pupal skin splits.

The head emerges first.

The young beetle has no spots.

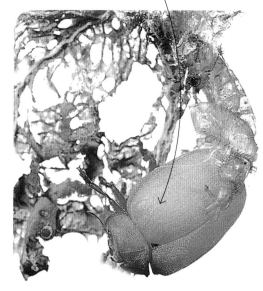

5 Resting

During the pupal stage, all the muscles, nerves, and other structures dissolve and new limbs, with new muscles and nerves, are formed. In the picture above, the adult beetle's yellow wing cases and the first segment of the thorax can be seen through the spiny skin of the pupa.

6 Ready to feed

The thin, spiny pupal skin splits along the underside, and the smooth young adult slowly emerges, head first.

7 No spots

The young beetle is yellow and has no spots, although the wing cases quickly harden. Before the beetle can fly, it needs to hold up its wing cases and expand its wings to allow them to dry. This process takes two to three hours.

8 One more pest

After about 24 hours, the adult spots appear on the wing cases, but the copper color takes about a week to develop fully. In 1918, the Mexican bean beetle was accidentally imported to the eastern United States and spread rapidly toward Canada. Today, it is a serious pest of bean crops in the US.

A complete metamorphosis has four stages: egg, larva, pupa and adult.

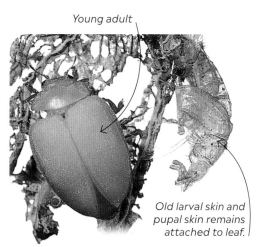

Young adult

Old larval skin and pupal skin remains attached to leaf.

From nymph to adult

Some insects, such as cockroaches, termites, and damselflies, go through a gradual transformation process known as incomplete metamorphosis. Their young, or nymphs, look like small versions of the adults. Very young nymphs have no wings, but older nymphs have "buds" on the thorax, inside which the adult wings develop. At each molt, these wing buds get longer until finally a nymph molts and an adult emerges.

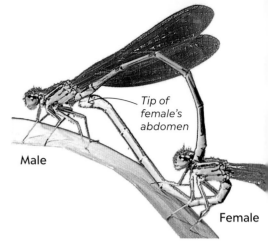

Tip of female's abdomen

Male

Female

Lovehearts

During mating, the male damselfly clasps the female's neck using the tip of his abdomen. The female then loops her abdomen forward in order to mate. They may fly together in this position for some time, often forming a heart shape with the male's head down at the tip and the female's head at the top of the heart.

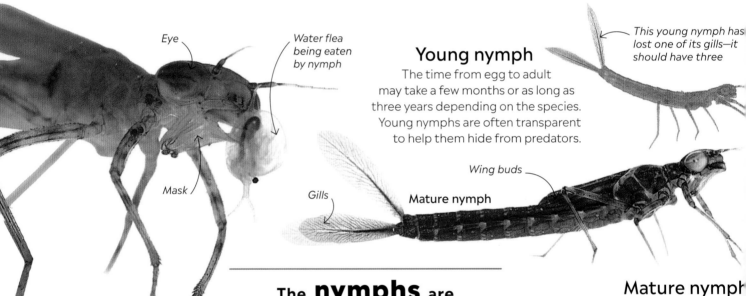

Eye

Water flea being eaten by nymph

Mask

This young nymph has lost one of its gills—it should have three

Young nymph

The time from egg to adult may take a few months or as long as three years depending on the species. Young nymphs are often transparent to help them hide from predators.

Wing buds

Gills

Mature nymph

Nymph prey

Damselfly nymphs have a special lower jaw called a mask that shoots out to capture prey.

The **nymphs** are **ferocious predators** and feed on larvae of other insects and on tadpoles.

Mature nymph

When fully grown, a nymph often uses camouflage to hide both from its prey and from predatory fish. Its wing buds can be seen extending from the thorax over the first three segments of the abdomen.

Earwigs

Female earwigs sometimes dig a small hole to lay their eggs in. They then stay with the eggs to protect them. Even when the young nymphs emerge, the female remains with them until they are ready to fend for themselves.

Gills

Dragonfly and damselfly nymphs absorb oxygen and get rid of carbon dioxide in the same way that fish do—by means of gills. But unlike a fish, the gills of a damselfly nymph are not on the head, but in the form of three fan-shaped structures on the tail.

The mature nymph crawls out of the water so that the adult can emerge.

The adult emerges

Although the damselfly nymph lives underwater, whereas the adult flies, the mature nymph has a similar structure to the adult. It has the flight muscles and deep thorax, but the body and wings need to grow, and the nymphal mask must be shed. These changes are prepared within the nymph underwater. Once in the air, it must change to an adult and fly quickly, usually in about two hours, or it will be eaten by some other animal.

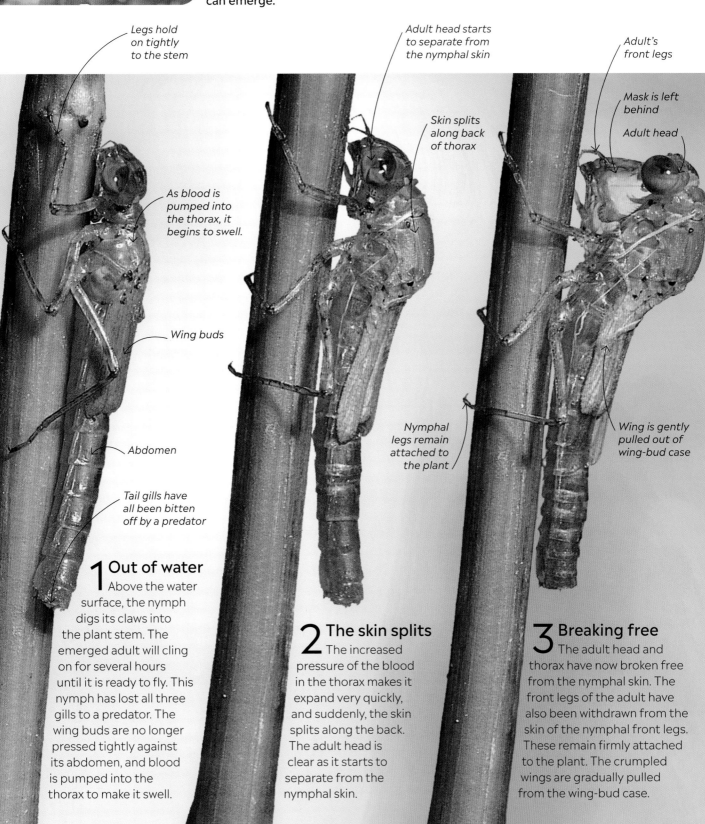

Legs hold on tightly to the stem

As blood is pumped into the thorax, it begins to swell.

Wing buds

Abdomen

Tail gills have all been bitten off by a predator

Adult head starts to separate from the nymphal skin

Skin splits along back of thorax

Nymphal legs remain attached to the plant

Adult's front legs

Mask is left behind

Adult head

Wing is gently pulled out of wing-bud case

1 Out of water

Above the water surface, the nymph digs its claws into the plant stem. The emerged adult will cling on for several hours until it is ready to fly. This nymph has lost all three gills to a predator. The wing buds are no longer pressed tightly against its abdomen, and blood is pumped into the thorax to make it swell.

2 The skin splits

The increased pressure of the blood in the thorax makes it expand very quickly, and suddenly, the skin splits along the back. The adult head is clear as it starts to separate from the nymphal skin.

3 Breaking free

The adult head and thorax have now broken free from the nymphal skin. The front legs of the adult have also been withdrawn from the skin of the nymphal front legs. These remain firmly attached to the plant. The crumpled wings are gradually pulled from the wing-bud case.

Continued on next page

Continued from previous page

Dragonflies

Dragonflies have a longer life cycle than damselflies—the larger species may take two to three years from egg to adult. The nymphs have complicated gills inside the abdomen through which water is pumped in and out. Adult dragonflies rest with their wings spread wide and are generally more active fliers than damselflies.

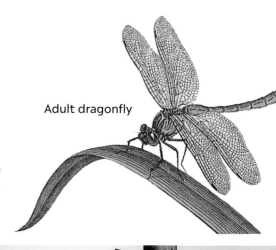

Adult dragonfly

Dragonfly nymphs

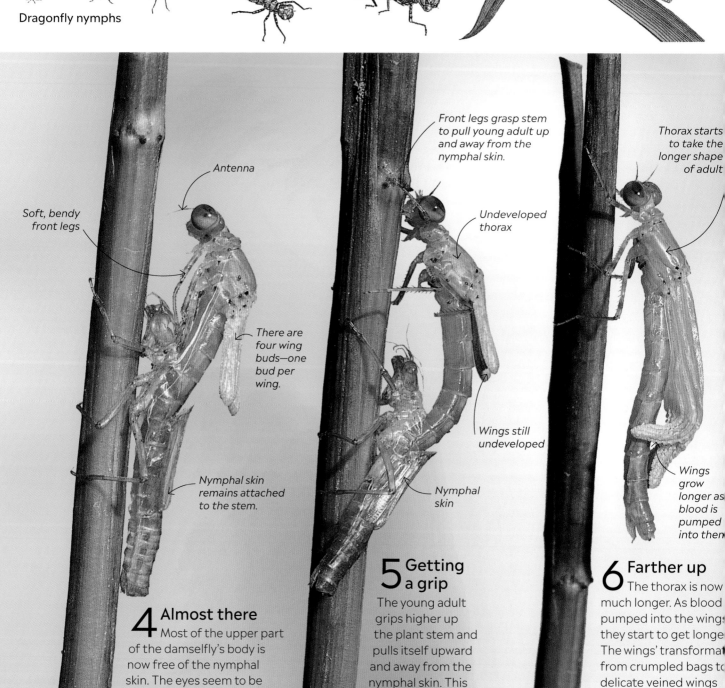

Antenna

Soft, bendy front legs

There are four wing buds—one bud per wing.

Nymphal skin remains attached to the stem.

4 Almost there
Most of the upper part of the damselfly's body is now free of the nymphal skin. The eyes seem to be hard and functional, but the front legs of the emerging adult are still soft and bendy. The four wing buds—one per adult wing—are still very small and compact.

Front legs grasp stem to pull young adult up and away from the nymphal skin.

Undeveloped thorax

Wings still undeveloped

Nymphal skin

5 Getting a grip
The young adult grips higher up the plant stem and pulls itself upward and away from the nymphal skin. This action enables it to free the tip of its abdomen. The thorax is still undeveloped and has not yet taken on its adult form.

Thorax starts to take the longer shape of adult

Wings grow longer as blood is pumped into them

6 Farther up
The thorax is now much longer. As blood is pumped into the wings, they start to get longer. The wings' transformation from crumpled bags to delicate veined wings is one of the most remarkable features of the incomplete metamorphosis of dragonflies and damselflies.

Damselflies

These delicate-looking insects are found near water. They have four similarly shaped, net-veined wings, which they hold above the body when resting. The damselfly shown below is a female of the species *Coenagrion puella*. The females of this species have a black back and brilliant green sides; the males have a blue back.

Close-up

This photograph shows the head of an adult male damselfly. It has large compound eyes and powerful chewing mouthparts.

After **damselflies** turn into **adults**, they **live** for only a **couple of weeks**.

Strong, chewing mouthparts

Legs seize and hold prey.

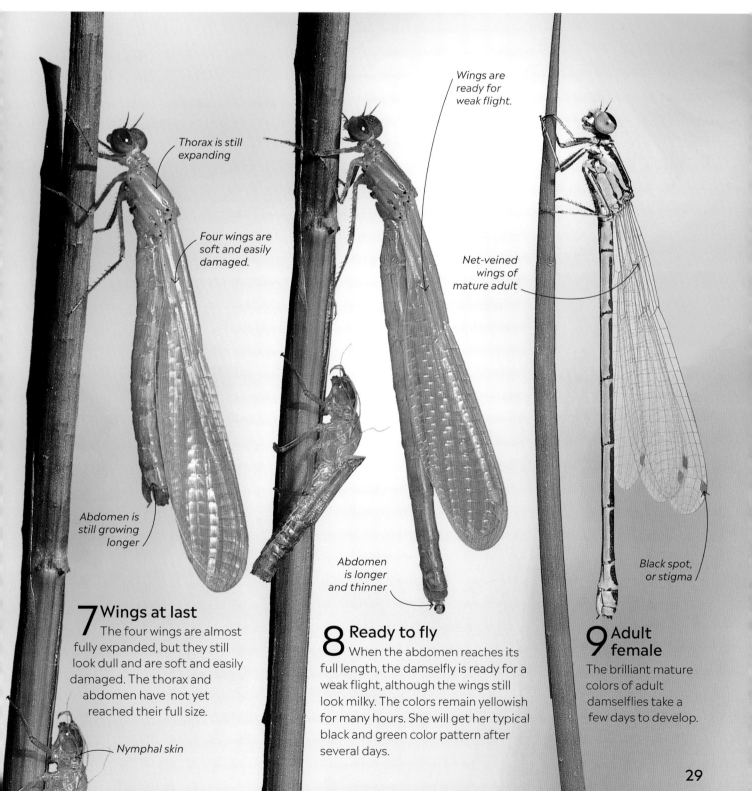

Wings are ready for weak flight.

Thorax is still expanding

Four wings are soft and easily damaged.

Net-veined wings of mature adult

Abdomen is still growing longer

Abdomen is longer and thinner

Black spot, or stigma

7 Wings at last

The four wings are almost fully expanded, but they still look dull and are soft and easily damaged. The thorax and abdomen have not yet reached their full size.

Nymphal skin

8 Ready to fly

When the abdomen reaches its full length, the damselfly is ready for a weak flight, although the wings still look milky. The colors remain yellowish for many hours. She will get her typical black and green color pattern after several days.

9 Adult female

The brilliant mature colors of adult damselflies take a few days to develop.

29

Beetles

There are at least 400,000 different kinds of beetles, living everywhere from snowy mountaintops to scorching deserts. All beetles undergo complete metamorphosis. Their eggs hatch into grubs, some of which feed and grow for several years before becoming adults. Adult beetles are the most heavily armored of all insects. They have tough front wings that meet in the middle to protect the more delicate hind wings, which they use for flying.

Goliath

The African Goliath beetle is the heaviest beetle in the world and one of the largest flying insects. The adults feed on fruit and can weigh up to 3.4 oz (100 g).

Goliathus cacicus

The females have grooved wing cases

Diving beetle

The great diving beetle is a voracious predator found in ponds and streams in Europe and northern Asia. It feeds on tadpoles and small fish. This female great diving beetle is resting on an oak leaf under the water.

Dytiscus marginalis

Leaf life

The Malayan frog beetle (far left) uses its large hind legs to clasp a female during mating. The South American species *Doryphorella langsdorfi* lives and feeds on leaves.

Malayan frog beetle (male)

Doryphorella langsdorfi

Froglike hind legs

Darwin's beetle

Jewel-like colors help conceal weevils on shiny green leaves

Lamprocyphus augustus

Pachyrhynchus species

Rostrum

Eupholus beccarii

Eupholus linnei

Hairs deter predators

Brachycerus fascicularis

Long running legs

Ground beetle

Tiger beetle

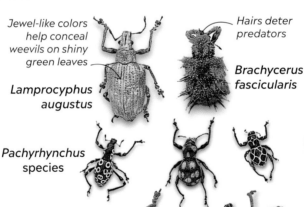

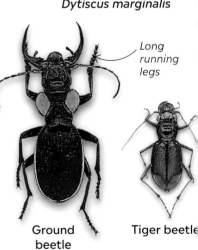

Darwin's beetle

It is said that this male stag beetle (*Chiasognathus grantii*) bit the English naturalist Charles Darwin when he visited Brazil. It probably uses its long, spiny jaws for defense.

Weevils

Weevils have a snout, or rostrum, with small biting jaws. Many are brilliantly colored and patterned. The middle three, from the Philippines, possibly mimic spiders.

Killer beetles

Ground beetles and the closely related tiger beetles hunt and kill smaller insects for food. This large African species (above left) scurries along the ground after its prey. The green tiger beetle (above right) is from Australia.

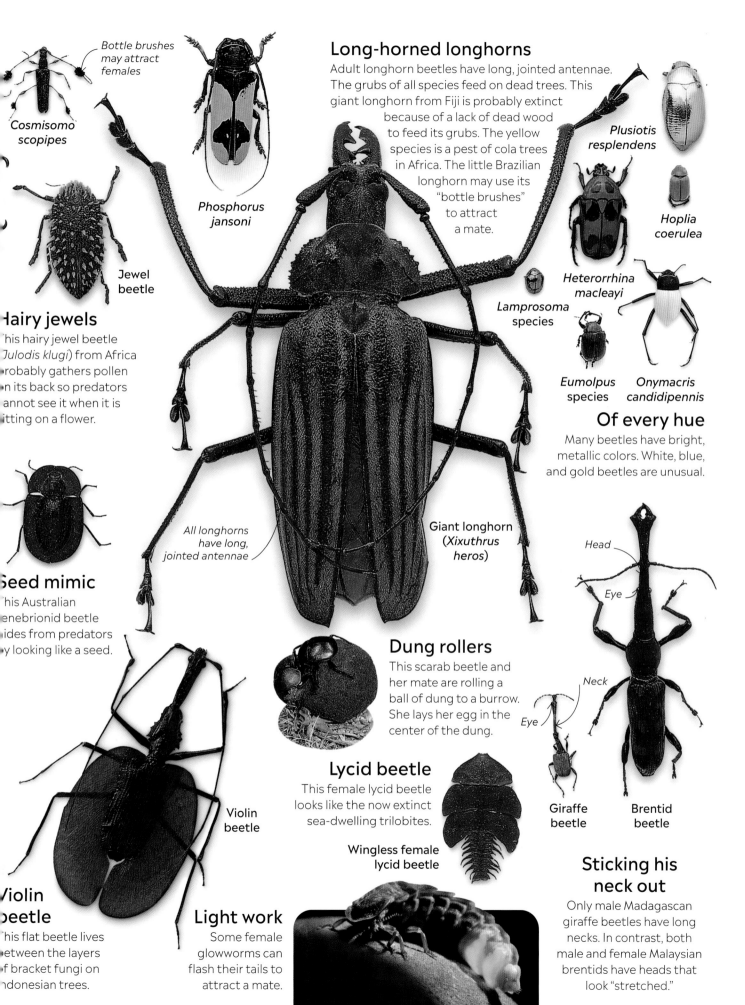

Bottle brushes may attract females

Cosmisomo scopipes

Phosphorus jansoni

Long-horned longhorns

Adult longhorn beetles have long, jointed antennae. The grubs of all species feed on dead trees. This giant longhorn from Fiji is probably extinct because of a lack of dead wood to feed its grubs. The yellow species is a pest of cola trees in Africa. The little Brazilian longhorn may use its "bottle brushes" to attract a mate.

Plusiotis resplendens

Hoplia coerulea

Heterorrhina macleayi

Lamprosoma species

Eumolpus species

Onymacris candidipennis

Of every hue

Many beetles have bright, metallic colors. White, blue, and gold beetles are unusual.

Jewel beetle

Hairy jewels

This hairy jewel beetle (*Julodis klugi*) from Africa probably gathers pollen on its back so predators cannot see it when it is sitting on a flower.

Seed mimic

This Australian tenebrionid beetle hides from predators by looking like a seed.

All longhorns have long, jointed antennae

Giant longhorn (*Xixuthrus heros*)

Head

Eye

Neck

Eye

Dung rollers

This scarab beetle and her mate are rolling a ball of dung to a burrow. She lays her egg in the center of the dung.

Lycid beetle

This female lycid beetle looks like the now extinct sea-dwelling trilobites.

Wingless female lycid beetle

Violin beetle

Giraffe beetle

Brentid beetle

Violin beetle

This flat beetle lives between the layers of bracket fungi on Indonesian trees.

Light work

Some female glowworms can flash their tails to attract a mate.

Sticking his neck out

Only male Madagascan giraffe beetles have long necks. In contrast, both male and female Malaysian brentids have heads that look "stretched."

Flies

A fly is an insect with two wings. Instead of hind wings, flies have a pair of small structures called halteres, which help them balance in flight. Flies have large compound eyes, as well as claws and pads on their feet so they can walk on any surface. Some kinds of flies help humans by pollinating crops. But many, like mosquitoes, are pests that spread diseases, such as malaria, and carry germs. All flies undergo complete metamorphosis. The grubs, or maggots, live mainly in water or in moist, rotting plant and animal tissue.

Wingless

This tiny bat fly (*Penicillidia fulvida*, above) has no wings. It lives in the fur of bats and feeds on blood. The female gives birth to a fully grown grub.

Ctenophora flaveolata

Crane flies

There are around 10,000 known species of crane fly, and the *Holorusia* species (below) from China is one of the largest. Others, such as *Ctenophora flaveolata* from Europe (above right), have shorter legs and can be spectacularly colored. Crane fly maggots have a tough covering and are often called "leather-jackets."

The world's biggest crane fly

An eye for an eye

The stalked eyes of this male fly (*Achias rothschildi*, right) from New Guinea are used to threaten other males with shorter eye stalks.

Eye

Stalk-eyed fly

Holorusia species

Halteres used for balancing

Beetle mimic

Celyphus hyacinthus

This small fly (*Celyphus hyacinthus*, left) from Malaysia looks remarkably like a beetle.

Green skin

Soldierfly

The green color of this South American soldierfly (*Hedriodiscus pulcher*, left) is caused by an unusual green pigment in the cuticle.

A fasting fly

The grubs of this South American fly (*Pantophthalmus bellardii*, below) bore into living wood. Little is known about the large adults, and it may be that they do not even feed.

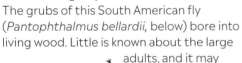

Housefly

Dung fly

Dung feeders

Dung flies are commonly seen on wet cow dung. Houseflies also breed on animal dung, as well as on decaying food. They spread many diseases.

Flesh eaters

When a mosquito carrying warblefly eggs feeds on a human, the eggs hatch and the larva bore under the human's skin. Bluebottles are common pests that breed in rotting meat and dead bodies and spread disease.

No eye stalks

This African fly (*Clitodoca fenestralis*) is related to the stalk-eyed fly from New Guinea. The patterned wings and red head may be important in courtship.

Human warblefly

Bluebottle

Drone flies

According to the Old Testament, Samson saw a swarm of bees in the dead body of a lion. The insects were almost certainly not bees, but yellow and black drone flies. These flies look like bees, but their larvae live and pupate in stagnant water.

Spider eater

The maggots of the *Lasia corvina* fly feed on tarantulas.

Long tongue for feeding on nectar

Flat flower-feeder

This Argentinian fly (*Trichophthalma philippii*) feeds on nectar.

Formosia moneta

Paradejeania rutiloides

A varied diet

This horsefly from Nepal feeds on blood and has a long tongue to sip nectar.

Short biting mouthparts

Tachinid flies

The maggots of tachinid flies feed on other living insects. The yellowish species (*Paradejeania rutiloides*) from America attacks moth caterpillars. The green species (*Formosia moneta*) from New Guinea feeds on scarab beetle larvae.

African bee fly

The maggots of this African bee fly feed on developing grubs in wasps' nests.

A slim profile

Like true bees, this bee fly from Java sips nectar. Its larvae feed on live moth caterpillars.

Philoliche longirostris

Syrphus torvus

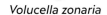

Volucella zonaria

Hover flies

Hover flies have an amazing ability to hang in the air almost motionless, then suddenly dart away at speed. Many species have yellow and black stripes and look like wasps or bees. The maggots of *Syrphus torvus* feed on greenfly. *Volucella zonaria* maggots scavenge for food beneath wasps' nests.

Bee-eating bee fly

This dotted bee fly (*Bombylius discolor,* left) from Europe resembles a bumblebee. Its maggots live in the nests of solitary bees and eat the bee larvae.

Blepharotes splendidissimus

Wing

Mallophora atra

Robberflies

These flies perch on suitable lookout points and attack other insects flying past. They can be pests around beehives, killing bees as they fly home. The large black species (*Mallophora atra*) from South America probably mimics carpenter bees. The male with plumed legs (*Pegesimallus teratodes*) is from Africa. The hornet robberfly (below) from Europe is a hornet mimic. *Blepharotes splendidissimus* from Australia is one of the largest robberflies.

Pegesimallus teratodes

Largest fly

This South American mydid fly (*Gauromydas heros,* right) is probably the largest in the world. The maggots live in ants' nests, feeding on beetles—which are themselves scavenging on the waste left by the ants.

Gauromydas heros

Leg

Asilus crabroniformis

Wing

Butterflies and moths

Butterflies and moths form a single group of around 200,000 species. Butterflies are mostly brightly colored and fly during the day, whereas the more subtly colored moths are usually nightfliers. Most butterflies have clubbed antennae, while those of moths are usually straight or feathery. Adult butterflies and moths feed on liquids, which they suck up through a long, coiled tube called a "proboscis."

Hooked antenna

Hesperia comma

Urbanus proteus

Butterfly or moth?

Skippers are butterflies that resemble moths in some ways. Like moths, they have thicker bodies and hooked antennae, unlike the club-shaped antennae of most butterflies

Nymphalid

The deep, intense blue of this nymphalid (*Asterope sapphira*) is caused by light striking the scales on its wings

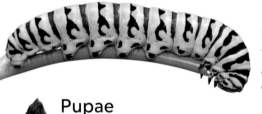

Caterpillars

The eggs of butterflies and moths hatch into caterpillars.

Don't eat me!

Red, yellow, and black colors often indicate that an insect is poisonous. Birds probably avoid this zygaenid moth (*Campylotes desgodinsi*) from India.

Pupae

When a caterpillar has eaten enough, it turns into a pupa. As soon as this splits open, the adult emerges.

Old lady moth

This old lady moth (*Mormo maura*) from Europe flies at night. During the day, its drab-colored wings conceal it on trees where it rests.

Declining numbers

Lappet moth (*Gastropacha quercifolia*) numbers have recently fallen by more than 50 percent in the UK as a result of habitat loss and other human-induced factors.

At rest, the lappet moth resembles dried oak leaves because of its wing shape and coloration

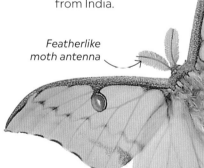

Featherlike moth antenna

Eyespot

Long tails will break off if caught

End of a tail

The eyespots on the wings of the African moon moth (*Argema mimosae*) probably divert predators away from the delicate body. Similarly, the long tails will break off when attacked. Its green color quickly fades to yellowish-white in daylight.

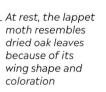

Jean-Henri Fabre

French entomologist Jean-Henri Fabre studied insects in the 19th century. Rather than collect dead specimens, he observed live insects in their natural habitat, noting their anatomy and behavior. Known as the father of entomology, his writings and paintings provide valuable insights into the insect world.

Clubbed antenna

Butterfly wings

utterflies rest with their wings olded together above their back. or this grayling (*Hipparchia emele*) from Europe, it also rovides excellent camouflage.

See-through wings

Some butterflies and moths, like this South American species (*Cithaerias esmeralda*), have see-through wings, making them difficult targets for predators.

Underside　　Upper side

Come in number 88!

These two South American 88 butterflies (*Diaethria marchalii*) are identical— the left one shows the underside of the right one.

Perfume for the lady

This colorful South American butterfly (*Agrias claudina sardanapalus*) feeds on rotting ruit. The males have bright yellow scent scales on the hind wings, which help attract the females.

Swallowtail butterflies

The swallowtails get their name from their extended hind wings, which often look like a swallow's forked tail. Due to its unusually clubbed hind wings, this common clubtail butterfly (*Pachliopta coon coon*) flies rather haphazardly and is often difficult to catch.

Butterflies on the move

Many butterflies undertake long migrations. In the fall, monarchs from all over North America migrate south, often over thousands of miles. Eastern populations winter in Mexico, and western ones in coastal California. In spring, they start their journey back north, laying eggs along the way so that successive generations move farther north.

Bugs

The word "bug" is often used to describe any crawling insect. But bugs are a special group of insects with a long, jointed feeding tube, specially adapted to piercing and sucking. The front wings of many bugs are hard and horned at the base, with thin, overlapping tips that protect the delicate hind wings. All bugs undergo incomplete metamorphosis, and young bugs look very similar to their parents, only without wings.

Who needs male bugs

Many aphids bear live young and can reproduce without the male.

Curved rostrum (feeding tube)

Hissing assassin

Assassin bugs, like this species (*Rhinocoris alluaudi*, left), can produce hissing sounds by rasping their curved feeding tube against a structure under their body.

Strong grasping front legs seize small water creatures.

Eye

Leafhoppers

This *Graphocephala fennahi* leafhopper feeds on rhododendron leaves. Other species cause damage to a wide range of plants.

Cuckoo-spit

This *Philaenus spumarius* froghopper nymph is producing "cuckoo-spit"—a froth that protects young froghoppers from drying out and from being eaten.

Bedbugs (enlarged)

Nighttime pests

The bedbug (*Cimex lectularius*) belongs to a small family of bloodsucking bugs, most of which live in the roosts and nests of bats and birds. They can live for several months without food.

Ground pearls (*Margarodes formicarum*)

Ground pearls

Many bugs are wingless and scarcely look like insects. These "ground pearls" are the shed skins of a group of plant-feeding bugs.

Unusual plant feeders

Some plant-feeding bugs have unusual legs, like the spiny legged bug *Thasus acutangulus*. Others have horns, such as *Ceratocoris horni*, or strange shapes, such as *Hemikyptha marginata*.

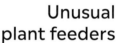

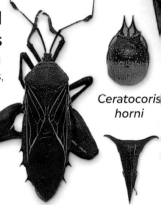

Ceratocoris horni

Thasus acutangulus

Hemikyptha marginata

Serenading cicadas

Cicadas, like this Indian species *Polyneura ducalis*, are known for the songs the males use to attract females. The nymphs live underground, sucking sap from plant roots.

Sap suckers

Many bugs, such as the rose aphid (*Macrosiphum rosae*, left) and the citrus mealybug (*Planococcus citri*, far left), feed on plant sap.

Deadly assassins

Assassin bugs are all predators. The *Gardena melanarthrum* species (below right) uses its long, slender legs to pick food off spiders' webs. The stoutly built *Centraspis* species (right) attacks more mobile prey, such as millipedes.

Assassin bug (*Platymeris biguttata*) feeding on a ground beetle

Assassin bug (*Centraspis* species)

Lantern bug in flight

Eyespots probably deter predators.

Assassin bug (*Gardena melanarthrum*)

Alligator eye

True eye

Alligator

Flying alligator

The front of the head of this lantern bug (*Fulgora servillei*, above) looks like an alligator's head, complete with teeth, nostrils, and eyes. The true eyes and antennae are low down at the back of the head. The bug lives in trees and is hard to see when sitting on branches.

Broad legs help bug swim.

Wings overlap.

Flying the flag

This sap-feeding coreid bug (*Bitta flavolineata*, right) waves the flaglike extensions on its legs, probably to distract predators from attacking its body.

Flags on hind legs are waved gently so a predator will attack these rather than the body.

Runibia decorata

Calliphara excellens

Chrysocoris sellatus

Underwater bugs

Giant waterbugs (*Lethocerus grandis*, above) are common throughout the tropics. They live underwater and eat snails or even small frogs and fish.

Change of diet

Young derbid bugs like this mothlike species (*Derbe longitudinalis*, above) feed on fungi, while the adults can be plant pests.

Shield bug (*Pycanum rubens*)

Young shield bugs look like tiny adults.

Shielding her young

Many species of shield bugs are brightly colored. The wings are protected by a huge shield that covers the hind part of the body. In some species, the female shields her eggs and young by sitting over them.

Flash colors

Many fulgorid bugs have brightly colored hind wings, like this Central American species (*Phrictus quinquepartitus*). The colors are probably flashed to startle predators.

The patterns of some shield bugs resemble tribal shields.

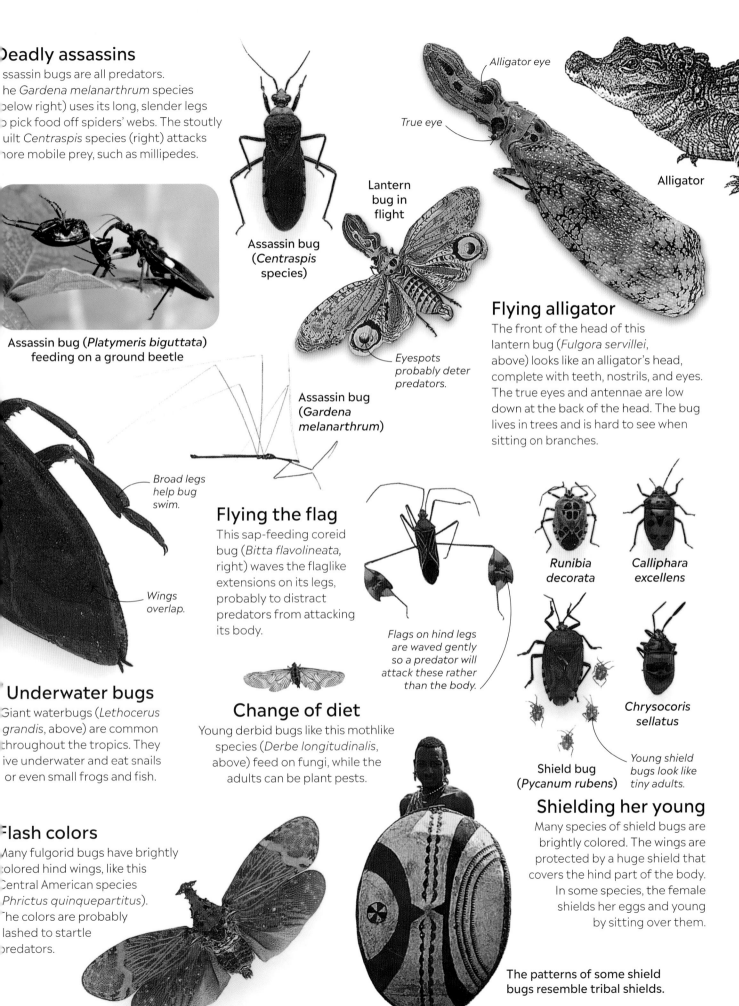

37

Wasps, bees, and ants

Wasps, bees, ants, and their relatives are one of the largest groups of insects. Besides sawflies, all wasps, bees, and ants have a narrow "waist." The egg-laying apparatus (ovipositor) in many female wasps and bees is modified as a painful sting. Several species of wasps, bees, and ants are "social" insects that live together in a nest they build themselves. Since early times, humans have kept bees for honey. Many wasp species are useful to farmers, as they kill the grubs and caterpillars that destroy crops. Wasps and bees are important pollinators for our fruit and vegetable crops.

👁 EYEWITNESS

Nikki Gammans
English entomologist Nikki Gammans works with the Bumblebee Conservation Trust in England. She has headed initiatives such as the short-haired bumblebee reintroduction project (2009-2022) and the ongoing Bee Connected aimed at working with local people to restore a more suitable habitat for rare bees in Kent. Her work has led to the return of many native bumblebee species in the region.

Tree wasps

In summer, tree wasp workers kill caterpillars to feed their grubs. In fall, when there are no grubs to feed, they become household pests, seeking sugary foods.

Male

Worker

Queen

Hornet

Hornets

The hornet (*Vespa crabro*) is the largest wasp in Europe. The queen begins her nest in spring. Her first eggs hatch into female workers that provide food for the grubs and for the queen herself. Males are produced later.

Spider killers

The tarantula hawk is the world's largest wasp. The female wasp paralyzes the spider with her sting, then lays an egg on its body. When the egg hatches, the grub has a ready supply of fresh spider meat.

Tarantula hawk

Parasitic bee

This large blue species (*Aglae caerulea*) lays its eggs in the nests made by orchid bees. The developing grub then eats the orchid bee grub as well as its food store.

Parasitic bee

Boring into trees

Female ichneumon wasps are parasitic—they lay their eggs on other insects, which the developing larvae consume. This female European rhyssine wasp (*Rhyssa persuasoria*) uses her long ovipositor to drill through wood to reach a live wood-boring sawfly grub, on which she lays her egg.

Biggest bee

This Asian carpenter bee is the world's largest bee. It makes nests in tunnels in rotting wood.

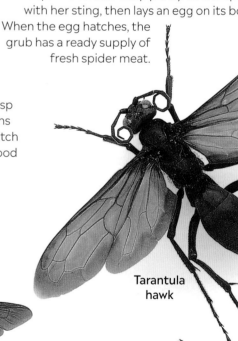

Bumblebees

Like honeybees, bumblebees are social insects and live in groups. This bilberry bumblebee (*Bombus monticola*) nests in a burrow in the ground, often close to bilberry bushes.

Osmia bicornis

Andrena cineraria

Solitary but living together

Solitary bees are so called because, unlike honeybees and bumblebees, they don't live in a single nest containing a queen and workers. Instead, many species live in colonies, each making a separate nest in a hole, but often in large groups.

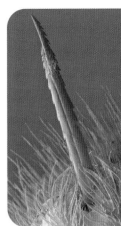

Sting

This is a magnified photograph of a sting—a modification of the ovipositor of many bees and wasps. It injects poison and causes a painful wound.

Parasitic wasps

The *Apanteles gratiosus* wasp lays its eggs on hairy caterpillars. After the grubs have eaten the inside of the caterpillar, they form cocoons on the surface.

Cocoons of *Apanteles* wasp

Chalinus imperialis larvae feed on beetle grubs in wood.

Chlorion lobatum

This giant wood wasp from Scandinavia is a pest of pine trees.

The *Cimbex femoratus* grub feeds on birch leaves.

Butterfly hunter

The *Editha magnifica* wasp from South America attacks butterflies as they sit on the ground. It stings them one at a time, bites off their wings, and stores the bodies in a burrow where it lays its eggs. The developing grubs feed on the butterflies' bodies until they are large enough to pupate.

Hunting wasps

Chlorion lobatum wasps sting crickets and then lay an egg on them. Once the wasp egg hatches, the grub feeds on the cricket's body.

Sawflies

Unlike other wasps, sawflies do not have a typical "waist." They owe their name to the sawlike blades of the egg-laying apparatus, or ovipositor, which the females use to insert eggs into plant tissues. The grubs, which often look like moth caterpillars, feed on plants. Sawflies are more common in the temperate parts of the world.

Ants

Ants live in colonies of up to 100,000 individuals. Their remarkably strong jaws can give a painful nip. When some species bite, they squirt formic acid from their abdomen into the wound—making it doubly painful.

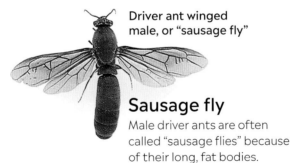

Driver ant winged male, or "sausage fly"

Sausage fly

Male driver ants are often called "sausage flies" because of their long, fat bodies.

Up to **20 million driver ants** travel in **long lines** when **hunting**.

Communication

Ants communicate by touch and smell. They have highly sensitive antennae that contain both touch and smell organs.

Driver ant queen

Driver ant workers

Driver ant

African driver ants form large colonies, but they have no permanent nests. They set up temporary camps while the queen lays eggs, then they move on, taking the developing grubs with them.

Largest ant

Dinoponera ants have the largest known workers. They live in small colonies but are solitary hunters.

Dinoponera grandis

Other insects

There are five main groups of insects: beetles, bugs, flies, wasps (including ants and bees), and butterflies and moths. However, there are another 25 similar but smaller groups, such as the cockroaches, earwigs, ant lions, mantises, dragonflies, grasshoppers, and stick insects. There are also several groups of much smaller species, including various types of lice.

Stephens Island weta
These large crickets (below) are now almost extinct.

Stephens Island weta (*Deinacrida rugosa*)

Living sticks

Stick insects usually have long, slender legs and antennae. During the day, they avoid predators by hanging almost motionless in shrubs and trees, looking just like another twig. At night, they move around to feed on leaves.

Slender, jointed leg

Antenna

Anchiale maculata from New Guinea

Wing

Eurycantha calcarata from Papua New Guinea

Grasping front legs sometimes make the insect look as though it is praying.

Praying mantis (*Sibylla pretiosa*) from Africa

Praying for food

Praying mantises feed on other insects, which they grasp in their specially adapted front legs.

Melanoplus bivittatus

Spines protect against attack.

Grasshopper's abdomen expands to act as a drum.

Strong hind legs enable fleas to jump great distances.

Mating fleas

Fleas

Adult fleas are all bloodsuckers. Each kind of flea prefers the blood of one kind of bird or animal. An animal flea will only attack a human if it is very hungry. The tiny, white flea larvae do not feed on blood, but on decaying material in nests and carpets.

Singing

Male grasshoppers, like this North American two-striped grasshopper (*Melanoplus bivittatus*, below left), produce sounds to attract females by rubbing their hind legs against their front wings. In contrast, crickets, such as the European great green bush-cricket (*Tettigonia viridissima*, left), "sing" by rubbing their two front wings together.

Tettigonia viridissima

Dragonflies and damselflies

Dragonflies (*Cordulegaster boltonii*, right) and damselflies (*Calopterygidae maculata*, far right) together make up one order of insects and feed on other insects. Their larvae are aquatic, whereas the adults (especially dragonflies) often feed away from the water.

Dragonflies rest with their wings open.

Damselflies rest with their wings together over their body.

Thread lacewing

This lacewing (*Nemoptera sinuata*, left) is related to the ant lion.

Cordulegaster boltonii

Calopterygidae maculata

Streamerlike hind wings trail behind to draw predator's attention away from vulnerable parts of the body.

Long, narrow wings with brown patterns

Adult Palpares libelluloides

Jaws

Ant lion (larva)

Ant lions

Ant lions are the larvae of the delicate four-winged *Palpares libelluloides*, which looks a bit like a damselfly. They dig funnel-shaped pits in loose sand. When an ant tumbles into the pit, the ant lion seizes it and sucks it to death.

👁 EYEWITNESS

Talash Huijbers
Kenyan businesswoman Talash Huijbers formed a company called InsectiPro in 2018 to produce soldier fly larvae for animal feed, and crickets as a protein source for humans on a large scale. This innovative idea will be important in providing a good protein source—and food security—for people in the future.

Strong fliers

The adults of this brightly colored species of lacewing (*Libelloides coccajus*, below) are strong fliers.

Biggest earwig

Libelloides coccajus

Cockroaches

These insects live just about everywhere and eat almost anything. Some are pests in the home, where their flat bodies allow them to hide in narrow spaces.

Megaloblatta longipennis, the largest flying cockroach

Giant earwig

This Australian earwig (*Titanolabis colossea*, left) is the largest in the world. Earwigs eat living and dead plants and animals and fold their hind wings under their short, dark front wings.

Living with plants

More than 300 million years ago, Earth's coal forests were home to insects such as dragonflies. The evolution of flowers and other types of plants encouraged the evolution of new insect species. Some evolved as pollinators; others fed on buds and seeds or on the different types of leaves and fruit that became available. Equally important was the evolution of insects that live on dead plants and restore nutrients to the soil.

Tunnel caused by moth larvae

Leaf miners
The larvae of the moth *Cameraria ohridella* feed on the tissue between the upper and lower surface of the horse chestnut leaf. As they eat, they tunnel out a shallow mine, leaving a trail of droppings behind. The larvae cause noticeable damage to the green leaves and may weaken the tree.

Oak processionary moth caterpillars
These oak processionary moth caterpillars are so called because they form lines as they move from branch to branch in search of fresh leaves. They can cause serious defoliation, or loss of leaves, if their numbers reach "plague" proportions.

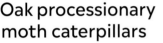

Plant deception
The flowers of some plants, such as the fly orchid (left), mimic a female fly or wasp to trick the male of the species into attempting to mate with it, picking up pollen in the process. This solitary wasp (*Argogorytes mystaceus*, above) then does the same with another plant and pollinates it.

Fly orchid flower looks like a female fly

Yellow specks are pollen grains.

Pollen grains on stamens of flower

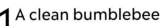

1 A clean bumblebee
Bees are essential to plants for carrying pollen from one flower to another, ensuring that seeds are produced. This bumblebee, attracted by the sweet scent of the dog rose, lands to feed on pollen and sugary nectar.

2 Dusted with golden pollen
As the bee sucks the nectar using its long tongue, its hairy coat picks up grains of pollen from the stamens.

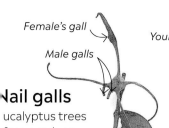

Nail galls

Eucalyptus trees often produce growths called galls, in which mealybug grubs develop. When mature, the female inside the gall is fertilized by a male through a tiny hole. Males develop in nail-like galls that often grow on a female gall.

Female's gall

Male galls

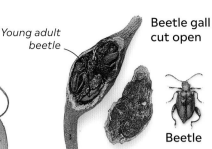

Young adult beetle

Beetle gall cut open

Beetle

Beetle gall

These *Sagra femorata* beetles developed inside the swollen stem of a climbing plant. The swelling started when the female beetle laid her eggs in the stem.

Rose galls

Rose galls are produced when a tiny gall wasp (*Diplolepis rosae,* below) lays her eggs on rosebuds in spring.

Cherries on oak trees

When the gall wasp (*Cynips quercusfolii*) lays an egg in the vein of an oak leaf, a cherry gall grows to protect the developing grub.

Young gall is white

Pistachio galls

These tubular galls are produced by pistachio trees around colonies of a particular aphid (*Baizongia pistaciae*) in the Mediterranean region.

Pistachio gall

Leaf

Safe and sound

Some caterpillars roll up a leaf, attach it with silk, then pupate safely hidden inside.

CHERRY GALL CYCLE

In winter, female gall wasps lay eggs on oak tree buds and galls develop. In late spring, grubs hatch, then they mate. The females lay eggs, and new cherry galls are produced.

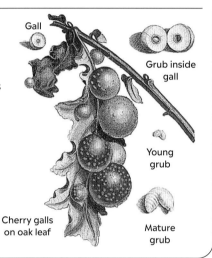

Gall

Grub inside gall

Young grub

Cherry galls on oak leaf

Mature grub

Pollen packed into tiny baskets on hind legs

Wind roses

Centuries ago in Persia, people believed that these pinkish galls came on the wind and called them "wind roses."

Marbles on oak trees

Oak marble galls are common on oak trees in Europe. They are produced by the females of a small gall wasp (*Andricus kollari*).

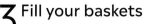

3 Fill your baskets

As the bee collects more and more pollen grains, it combs them from its body and packs them into the hairy pollen baskets on its hind legs. It goes on to visit several flowers, transferring pollen and ensuring reproduction.

Currant gall cut in half

Oak currants

In spring, female gall wasps (*Neuroterus quercusbaccarum*) lay eggs on oak catkins, producing currant galls. The grubs hatch and, in summer, after mating, the females lay eggs on oak leaves. A flat, reddish cushion called a spangle gall forms around each egg. In spring, an all-female generation of wasps emerges and the cycle begins again.

Hide and **seek**

Insects are eaten by many other animals, including birds, bats, frogs, lizards, and shrews. Many insects themselves hunt and kill other insects for food, and some insects are even eaten by people. With this range of predators, it is not surprising that many insects have developed unusual colors, patterns, and shapes to protect themselves. Some insects have mottled wings to match the color of tree bark. Leaf and stick insects are so well disguised as leaves and twigs that they are ignored by would-be predators.

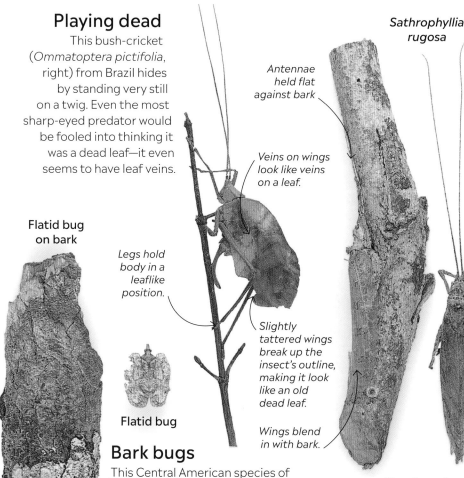

Playing dead

This bush-cricket (*Ommatoptera pictifolia*, right) from Brazil hides by standing very still on a twig. Even the most sharp-eyed predator would be fooled into thinking it was a dead leaf—it even seems to have leaf veins.

Flatid bug on bark

Sathrophyllia rugosa

Antennae held flat against bark

Veins on wings look like veins on a leaf.

Legs hold body in a leaflike position.

Slightly tattered wings break up the insect's outline, making it look like an old dead leaf.

Wings blend in with bark.

Flatid bug

Bark bugs

This Central American species of flatid bug (*Flatoides dealbatus*) sits on the bark of trees, where its light brown coloring makes it difficult to see. Some species are see-through, or translucent, while others have mottled brown and gray patches to blend in with lichen-covered trees.

Bark mimic

When it sits pressed closely against a small branch, this grayish-brown bush-cricket (*Sathrophyllia rugosa*) from India looks just like a piece of bark.

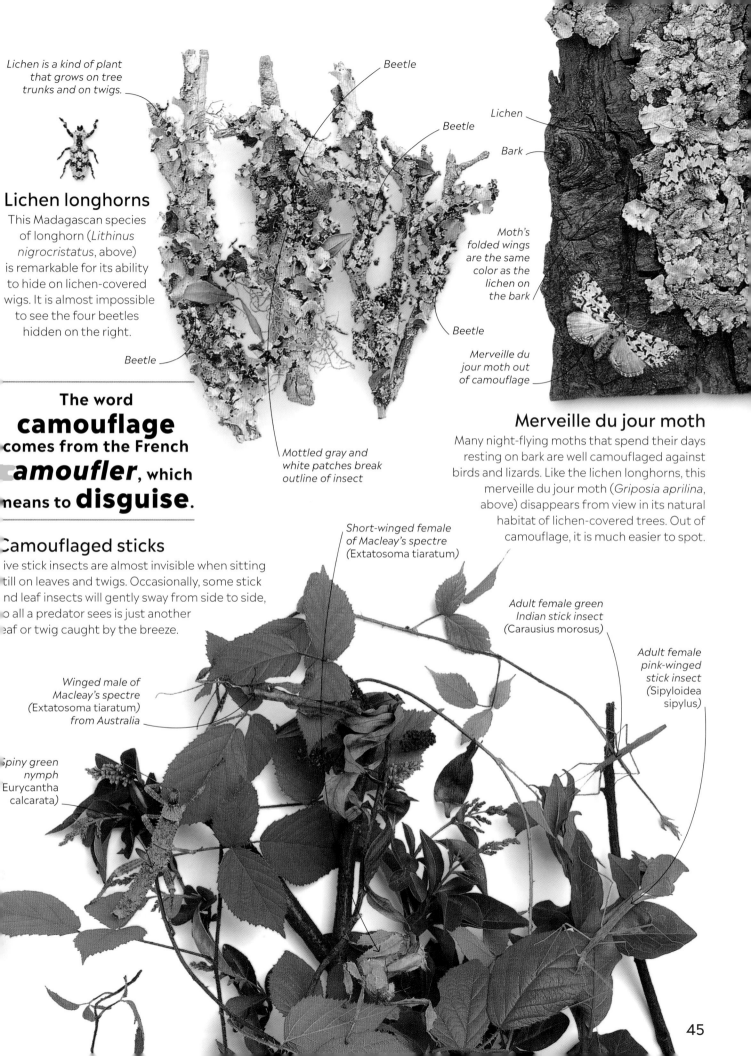

Lichen is a kind of plant that grows on tree trunks and on twigs.

Beetle

Beetle

Lichen

Bark

Lichen longhorns

This Madagascan species of longhorn (*Lithinus nigrocristatus*, above) is remarkable for its ability to hide on lichen-covered wigs. It is almost impossible to see the four beetles hidden on the right.

Moth's folded wings are the same color as the lichen on the bark

Beetle

Merveille du jour moth out of camouflage

Beetle

The word camouflage comes from the French camoufler, which means to disguise.

Mottled gray and white patches break outline of insect

Merveille du jour moth

Many night-flying moths that spend their days resting on bark are well camouflaged against birds and lizards. Like the lichen longhorns, this merveille du jour moth (*Griposia aprilina*, above) disappears from view in its natural habitat of lichen-covered trees. Out of camouflage, it is much easier to spot.

Camouflaged sticks

ive stick insects are almost invisible when sitting till on leaves and twigs. Occasionally, some stick nd leaf insects will gently sway from side to side, o all a predator sees is just another eaf or twig caught by the breeze.

Short-winged female of Macleay's spectre (Extatosoma tiaratum)

Adult female green Indian stick insect (Carausius morosus)

Adult female pink-winged stick insect (Sipyloidea sipylus)

Winged male of Macleay's spectre (Extatosoma tiaratum) from Australia

Spiny green nymph (Eurycantha calcarata)

Avoiding predators

Hiding from predators is the key to survival for many insect species. Some use camouflage to blend in with their surroundings. Others protect themselves with clearly visible spines; bright, flashing colors; strong, biting jaws; or powerful, kicking legs. Some harmless insects look and behave like poisonous or stinging creatures, so predators will mistake them for the real thing. Hungry predators learn to leave unsavory insects alone and avoid anything that could give them a painful bite or sting.

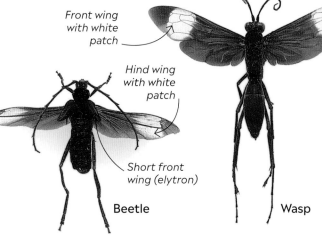

Front wing with white patch

Hind wing with white patch

Short front wing (elytron)

Beetle

Wasp

Beetles that mimic wasps

Many longhorn beetles mimic poisonous or stinging insects or develop remarkable camouflage to hide from predators. It is almost impossible, at first glance, to tell the difference between this Borneo longhorn beetle (*Nothopeus fasciatapennis*, above left) and the wasp it is mimicking (*Hemipepsis speculifer*, above right).

Antlike waist

Three parts of insect's body joined to look like two parts of spider's body

Spiderlike legs

Ant

Beetle

Ant mimic

This harmless African ground beetle (*Eccoptoptera cupricollis*) avoids predators by looking remarkably like a velvet ant (*Mutillidae*), which has a painful sting.

Spider mimic

This New Guinea weevil (*Arachnopus gazella*, above) runs around on the bark of trees looking just like a small spider.

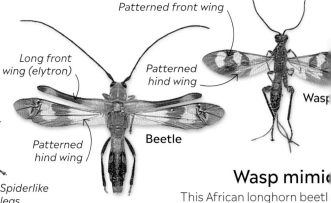

Patterned front wing

Long front wing (elytron)

Patterned hind wing

Patterned hind wing

Beetle

Wasp

Wasp mimic

This African longhorn beetle (*Nitocris patricia*, above left) has long, thin wing cases that, when closed, give the beetle a "wasp waist." The wasp it mimics (*Paracollyria* species, above right) attacks beetle grubs in plant stems.

Hornet mimic

Many insects, such as hover flies, look like wasps. But this sesiid moth (*Sesia apiformis*, below) is a remarkable mimic of the common hornet, known for its painful sting.

Furry legs

Bee ware!

When this moth (*Melittia gloriosa*, left) holds its furry legs against its abdomen, it looks like a large, hairy bee. Predators leave it alone for fear of being stung.

Hollow, peanutlike "head" to scare away predators

Fulgora laternaria

Eyespot

Yellow and brown stripes on the body

Transparent wings

Warning eyes

Various insects, like this fulgorid bug, have eyelike patterns on their hind wings. These are usually concealed when at rest. But when disturbed, the large "eyes" are flashed, giving the insect an opportunity to escape from its surprised predator.

Snake in the grass

Some caterpillars trick predators into thinking they are poisonous snakes. When alarmed, this Sphinx hawkmoth caterpillar (*Hemeroplanes triptolemus*) rears its head and inflates its thorax to look like a snake's head.

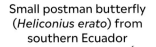

False snake eye

Small postman butterfly (*Heliconius erato*) from southern Ecuador

Decticus verrucivorus

Feeding, not fighting

This wart-biter is a bush-cricket with powerful jaws for eating hard seeds and insects—and for fending off predators.

Small postman butterfly (*Heliconius erato*) from western Brazil

Rings of mimics

Some butterflies feed on rather poisonous plants. As a result, they taste unpleasant and are avoided by insect-eating birds. Different species may take advantage of this by mimicking each other's colors. These six butterflies represent two species from three different parts of South America.

Small postman butterfly (*Heliconius erato*) from southern Brazil

Postman butterfly (*Heliconius melpomene*) from southern Ecuador

Postman butterfly (*Heliconius melpomene*) from western Brazil

Postman butterfly (*Heliconius melpomene*) from southern Brazil

1 Warning weta

As the wildlife in New Zealand developed without any mammals, a group of crickets called weta filled the role of the ground-living predators, eating a diet similar to that of shrews. These huge insects are now almost extinct.

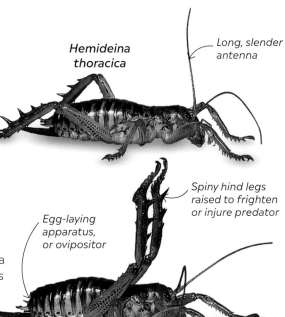

Hemideina thoracica

Long, slender antenna

Spiny hind legs raised to frighten or injure predator

Egg-laying apparatus, or ovipositor

2 Stick 'em up!

When disturbed, this species raises its hind legs into a threatening posture. The spines on the legs can cause a nasty wound when the insect kicks.

47

Mayfly
adult

A watery life

In order to breathe, water insects either swim to the surface for air or extract air from the water like fish. Some, such as dragonflies and many true flies, take advantage of the food supplies in water for their feeding and growing phase. As adults, they become winged and independent of water. Others spend their entire life cycle in water.

Skating
Pond skater
feed o
drownin
insect

Prey is held in front four legs

Oarlike hind legs

Sucking mouthparts

Eye

Silvery film of air

Air film
The silvery undersid of a saucer bug (left is caused by a film c air trapped beneat tiny hair

Pincerlike legs

Surface hunters
Water boatmen (*Notonecta glauca*, above) are predatory bugs that swim upside-down just beneath the surface, attacking other insects that have fallen in. They come to the surface to breathe.

Strong, pincerlike front legs

Saucer bugs
Saucer bugs (*Ilyocoris cimicoides*, above) have strong front legs for grasping their prey.

Air is stored beneath the wings

Fringes on legs propel beetle through water

Gills extract oxygen from water

Strong, grasping front legs

Predatory damsel
Damselfly nymphs (left) breathe through external gills on the tip of the abdomen.

Suckerlike pads used in mating

Segmented antenna

Giant water bug
This giant water bug (above), shown smaller than life-size, was drawn by Maria Merian in 1700.

Caddis fly larva
Many caddis fly larvae spin a tube of silk onto which they stick stones, sand, or bits of plant for camouflage.

Diving beetles
Great diving beetles (*Dytiscus marginalis*, above) are fierce predators. Like water boatmen, they store air under their wings.

Water beetle pupa
The larva of the great diving beetle (below right) crawls out of the pond and burrows into damp soil, where it pupates.

Pieces of plant

Sticks and stones

Caddis fly larvae

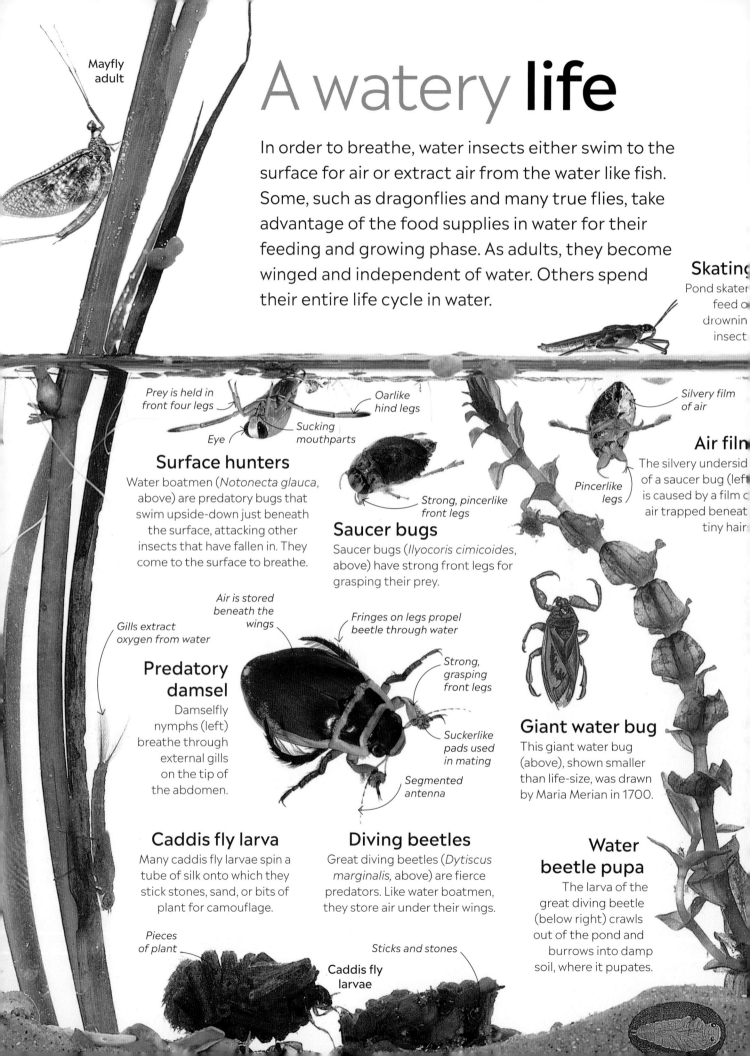

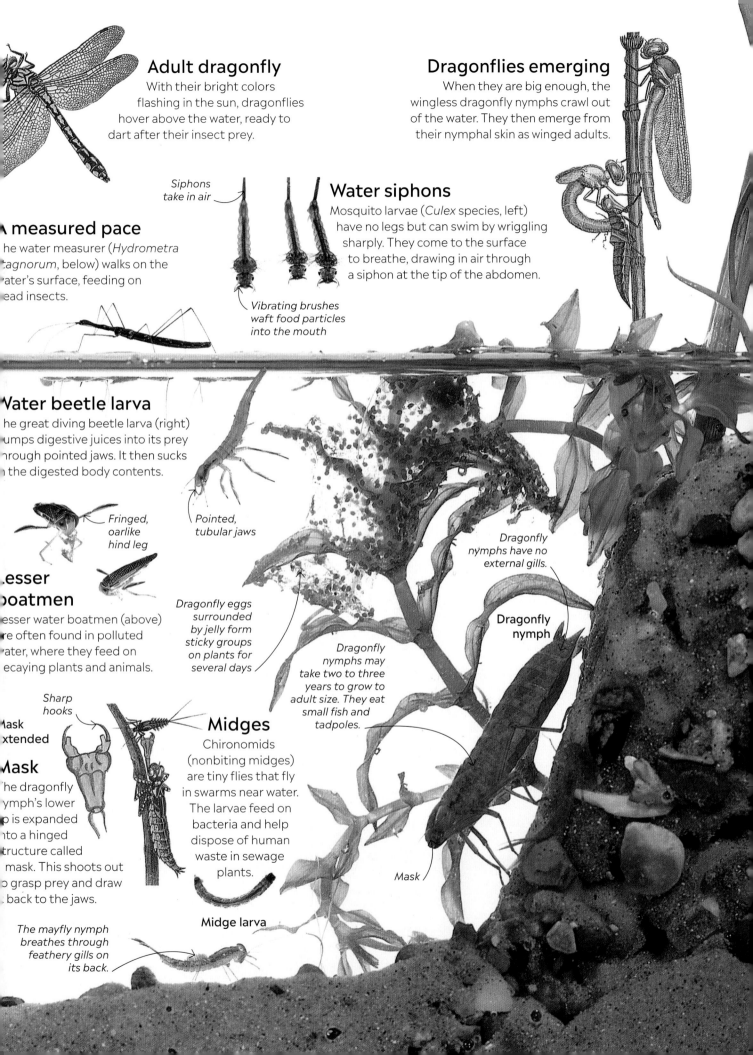

Adult dragonfly

With their bright colors flashing in the sun, dragonflies hover above the water, ready to dart after their insect prey.

Dragonflies emerging

When they are big enough, the wingless dragonfly nymphs crawl out of the water. They then emerge from their nymphal skin as winged adults.

Siphons take in air

Water siphons

Mosquito larvae (*Culex* species, left) have no legs but can swim by wriggling sharply. They come to the surface to breathe, drawing in air through a siphon at the tip of the abdomen.

A measured pace

The water measurer (*Hydrometra stagnorum*, below) walks on the water's surface, feeding on dead insects.

Vibrating brushes waft food particles into the mouth

Water beetle larva

The great diving beetle larva (right) pumps digestive juices into its prey through pointed jaws. It then sucks in the digested body contents.

Fringed, oarlike hind leg

Pointed, tubular jaws

Dragonfly nymphs have no external gills.

Lesser boatmen

Lesser water boatmen (above) are often found in polluted water, where they feed on decaying plants and animals.

Dragonfly eggs surrounded by jelly form sticky groups on plants for several days

Dragonfly nymphs may take two to three years to grow to adult size. They eat small fish and tadpoles.

Dragonfly nymph

Sharp hooks

Mask extended

Mask

The dragonfly nymph's lower lip is expanded into a hinged structure called a mask. This shoots out to grasp prey and draw it back to the jaws.

Midges

Chironomids (nonbiting midges) are tiny flies that fly in swarms near water. The larvae feed on bacteria and help dispose of human waste in sewage plants.

Mask

The mayfly nymph breathes through feathery gills on its back.

Midge larva

Building a **nest**

The nests of the common wasp (*Vespula vulgaris*) are started by a single queen working on her own. She builds each nest from chewed-up wood fibers and lays her eggs inside. The emerging grubs become the first workers—they expand the nest and forage for food so that the queen can stay in the nest to lay more eggs.

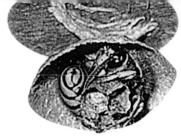

The start

The common wasp queen starts a nest by building a short stalk with a cap, covering a comb of four or five cells. She lays one egg at the bottom of each cell.

White paper envelopes are made from fibers of wood, which the queen chews and mixes with saliva to make a sort of "paper."

New envelope is built down and around older envelopes.

Stalk

Entrance to the nest is small to protect the larvae inside and to help control the temperature and humidity.

1 Insulating layers
The queen builds a series of envelopes around her small comb to insulate the larvae from cold winds. The nests of the common wasp are always built with the entrance at the bottom, unlike some tropical wasps' nests.

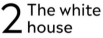

2 The white house
This queen has found a source of nesting material that is almost white. She chews away some wood fibers to make the "paper" from which she builds the nest.

3 Keeping guard
The nest entrance is now just a small hole. This is easier to defend from other insects, including other queens who might try to take over the nest.

Expert builder
The queen uses her antennae to measure the envelopes and cells of her nest.

Caring for the eggs
When the eggs hatch, the queen must collect food for her grubs as well as more material to extend the nest walls.

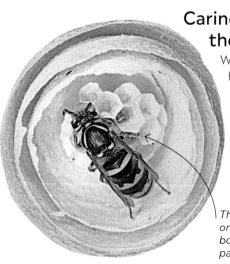

The queen lays one egg at the bottom of each paper cell.

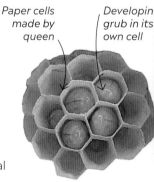

Paper cells made by queen

Developing grub in its own cell

Larvae
On their rich diet of chewed insects and caterpillars, the grubs grow quickly. The time from egg to adult is usually about five weeks.

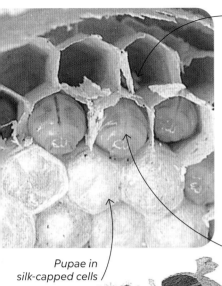

Egg at bottom of cell

Grubs with caps on

Just before the larvae pupate, they spin their own silken cap to close their cell. A few days later, the first set of workers emerges.

Pupae in silk-capped cells

Growing larva

 EYEWITNESS

Norina Vicente

Norina Vicente is a researcher at the Gorongosa National Park in Mozambique. She is part of a team that has documented more than 200 ant species—some unique to that part of the world. She uses macrophotography to create greater awareness and appreciation for the insect world.

Darker speckles on walls may be the result of some of the workers having fed on treated wood.

Different types of wood, making the paper multicolored

4 Change of color

The first workers start to collect wood fibers from many different sources, so the "paper" they make is often multicolored. Inside the nest, the old paper envelopes are chewed away to make room for larger combs of cells.

5 How many wasps?

A large nest may contain more than 500 adult wasps in summer. Between spring and fall, it will produce several thousand individuals, most of whom die from exhaustion.

Workers digging to make more space for the nest to grow

Underground nests

The common wasp often builds nests underground. As the nest grows, the workers have to dig away soil and stones to provide more room.

6 The next generation

In summer, the wasps build several larger cells. The grubs in these cells are given extra food. These larger grubs develop into males and queens, which fly from the nest and mate.

The worker wasp continues enlarging the nest.

Insect architects

Wasps, bees, ants, and termites build a wide range of nests to protect their young. The simplest is a burrow in the soil made by a solitary wasp. The most complex is made by termites and contains millions of workers and a single queen. Some nests, like those built by common wasps and honeybees, are started by a single queen. Others are started by swarms of female wasps, sometimes with several queens.

Long and thin

Ropalidia wasps build simple, open nests. Each consists of only a few cells hanging from a central stalk. The female lays a single egg in each cell and feeds the grubs as they develop.

Mud vase

Oriental *Stenogaster* wasps produce attractive vaselike nests made of mud and plant fibers. Each nest is built by a solitary female.

Leafy nest

Protopolybia sedula, a South American wasp species, builds a nest of up to 10 vertical combs between the leaves of a plant.

Vertical combs

Leaf

Vaselike shape

Walls are made largely of hardened mud picked up wet from the sides of streams.

Hole where branch was

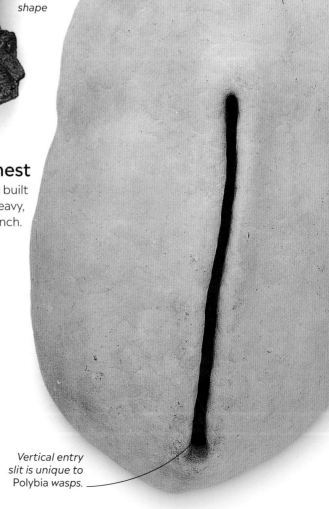

Clay nest

The nest of *Polybia singularis* is built largely of mud. As each nest is so heavy, it must be hung from a stout branch.

Vertical entry slit is unique to Polybia wasps.

Paper cones

The cylindrical nests of the South American *Chartergus globiventris* wasp have a small entry hole at the bottom. The nests vary in size from about 2 in (5 cm) long and 1.2 in (3 cm) wide to 3 ft (100 cm) long and 6 in (15 cm) wide. The largest nests contain many thousands of wasps with several egg-laying queens.

Branch supporting nest

Entrance hole

Hole at the center of each level allows wasps to move from floor to floor

Papier-mâché walls made of plant fibers, which the wasps collect and chew into a paste

Entrance hole

Carton nest

The nest above has been cut in half to show the inside. It is built from plant fibers, which the adult wasps collect and chew into a paste like papier-mâché. They build several layers of combs to rear their young, with a hole at the center of each layer so they can easily move from "floor" to "floor."

Spiny nest

The *Polybia scutellaris* wasp from Argentina and southern Brazil makes its nest from chewed plant fibers. The outer envelope is covered with hard, papery spines.

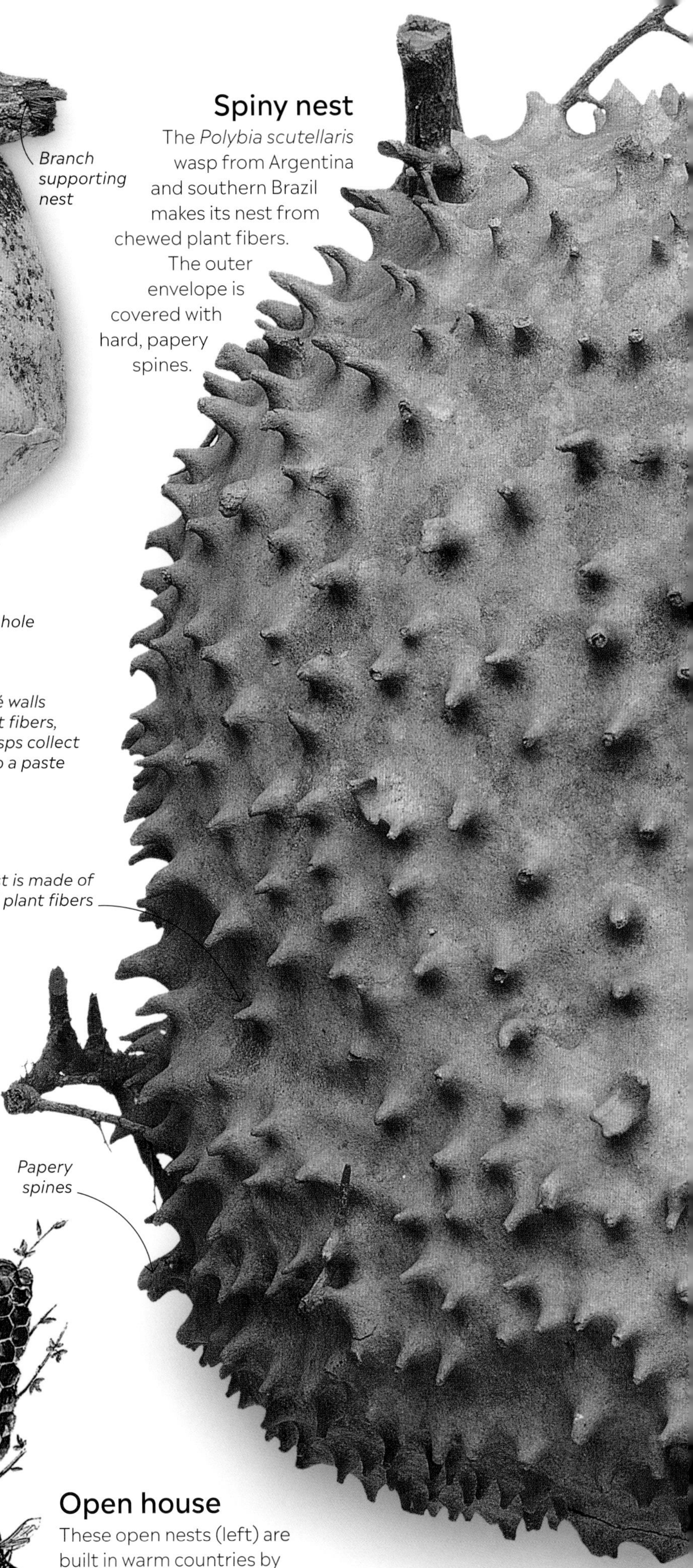

Nest is made of chewed plant fibers

Papery spines

Open house

These open nests (left) are built in warm countries by *Polistes* wasps.

Continued on next page

Continued from previous page

Nest of *Polybia scutellaris* from South America

Home protection

Apoica pallida wasps build simple open nests (right and above) with one comb of cells. The upper surface is protected by a conelike outer envelope made from plant fibers. The lower surface is protected by rows of wasps, all facing outward to ward off predators.

Brood cells containing developing grubs

Drummers' home

This simple nest with a single comb (right) is produced by a swarm of wasps that is thought to include several queens. These metallic blue wasps (*Synoeca surinama*) are among the largest social wasps in South America. They fly quietly, but when annoyed, they drum on the inside of their nest to produce a warning sound.

Spiny outer casing is made of chewed plant fibers

Entrance to nest

Winter protection

Some *Polybia scutellaris* nests, such as the one on the left, have been known to exist for 30 years. The thick, spiny envelope may be important in protecting the wasps through the cooler winters of southern South America.

Mouthlike entrance

54

Termites

The biggest and most complex insect societies are built by termites. The nests of some species, like the west African *Macrotermes bellicosus* (right), house up to 5 million termites. Nests usually have a single queen who lays all the eggs and a single king who fertilizes them all. In a really big nest, a queen and king may live for 15 years, and for much of her life, the queen will lay one egg every three seconds. She lives in a special chamber, ed constantly by the numerous workers. Large soldier ermites guard the many covered trails radiating ut of the nest, along which the workers bring ll the food needed for the colony.

Termite castes

) *Macrotermes* queen; 2) worker; 3) soldier; -) young nymph; 5) short-winged nymph;) long-winged nymph; 7) male; 8) young emale; 9) egg-laying female.

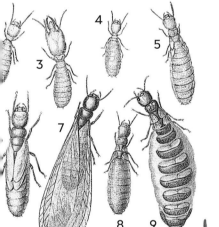

Air-conditioned city

This towering mound is really a ventilation chimney through which hot air from the nest can escape. Beneath the tower is a cave about 9 ft (3 m) in diameter, housing the nursery galleries, the queen's cell, and the fungus gardens that the termites cultivate for food. Water is obtained from deep cavities below the main cave.

Nest of
*Macrotermes
bellicosus*

Tree termites

Many termites build nests in trees, although these are usually connected to other parts of the same colony either underground or in other trees. Termites make communicating galleries with roofs by sticking soil particles together, or they tunnel in wood or underground.

Mysterious umbrellas

No one really knows the function of these umbrella nests of the African *Cubitermes* (right). A nest starts hidden underground. Then one or more columns may suddenly be built, and up to five caps may be added to each one.

Nest of *Cubitermes*

Walls are made from tiny pellets of earth cemented together with saliva

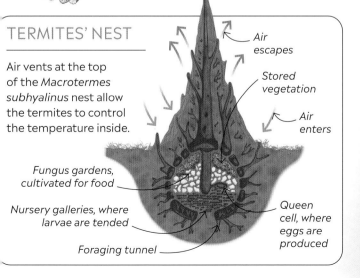

TERMITES' NEST

Air vents at the top of the *Macrotermes subhyalinus* nest allow the termites to control the temperature inside.

Air escapes

Stored vegetation

Air enters

Fungus gardens, cultivated for food

Nursery galleries, where larvae are tended

Queen cell, where eggs are produced

Foraging tunnel

Social ants

Most ant species live and work together in big colonies, often building complex nests in which to rear their young. Each nest is begun by a single queen, who lays all the eggs; there is no king. Ant species vary greatly. There are solitary and parasitic species, ants that rear workers from other nests as slaves, and "cuckoo" queens that enter nests and persuade the workers to kill their queen so they can raise her brood.

Wood ant[s]

In forests, wood ants are important insec[t] predators, and a big colony will collec[t] thousands of insects in one day. A large nes[t] may contain 100,000 ants with sever[al] queens, and it can last for many year[s]

Leaf-cutter ant[s]

A colony of leaf-cutter ants consumes a vas[t] quantity of leaves. These tropical America[n] leaf-cutter ants (*Atta cephalotes*) have cut ou[t] pieces of leaves and flowers and are carryin[g] them back to their nest. Here, they are cut up int[o] smaller pieces and used to grow a kind of fungu[s] on which the ants feed. The nest is usuall[y] underground and has special air conditioning t[o] ensure that the temperature and humidit[y] remain almost constant. A large nest may b[e] several yards across and will house several fungu[s] gardens and separate brood chamber[s]

The leaves are carried into the nest and used as a basis for growing a kind of fungus on which the ants feed.

The ants in the nest cut the leaves into smaller pieces and fertilize the fungus gardens with their waste.

The fungus flourishes only if attended to by the ants—if neglected, it will quickly die.

Bits of leaf are left at the entrance of the nest for the gardener ants to pick up and drag inside.

Ants returning to collect more leaves

An ant can carry a piece of leaf more than twice its size.

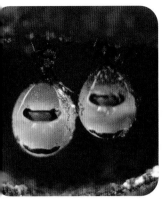

Honeypot ants

In semidesert areas, ants have found a unique way of surviving in the dry season. In the wet season, they feed some of their workers with water and nectar, who then store the extra food in their abdomens. They cannot move, but hang upside down in the nest as living larders, for use by the rest of the colony.

Weaver ants

Weaver ants build nests in trees by "sewing" together groups of large leaves. A row of worker ants pulls two leaves together. More workers, each holding a live ant larva in their jaws, sew the leaves together using strands of silk produced by the larva's salivary glands. The finished nest (above right) is a ball of leaves.

aws

Antenna

Ball-and-socket joint allows movement in all directions.

Eye

he shape of
n ant's jaws depends
n the food it eats.
ost ants are
redators, with long,
ointed jaws. This
sian tree-living
nt has simple jaws,
ith a few teeth
or feeding on soft
sects and honeydew.

Sense hairs

Toothed jaws for gripping food

Palps for sensing and manipulating food

These leaf-cutter ants are cutting out pieces of leaf to carry to their nest.

Weight lifters

Ants can lift objects that weigh more than they do. If threatened, the ants' first priority is to carry the brood to safety. The white objects in this photograph (above) are pupae, each with an almost mature adult inside.

leafy trail

rails of leaves can often be seen during
he day as the ants cross footpaths on the
oute back to the nest. Outward-bound
orkers can be seen stopping to encourage
heir colleagues.

Homeward-bound workers

Fair-weather workers

Leaf-cutter ants do not collect leaves when it is raining, and if a heavy shower occurs while they are out cutting, the leaves are usually dropped outside the nest. Wet leaves may upset the delicate balance inside the fungus gardens and endanger the colony's food supply.

Honeybees and **hives**

People have collected honey from the nests of bees for many centuries. The oldest record is a cave painting in Spain, nearly 9,000 years old, which shows a figure apparently taking honey from a nest on a cliff. In a modern domestic hive, there are three types of honeybees (*Apis mellifera*): one queen, a fertile, mated female who lays all the eggs—sometimes over 1,000 a day; a few hundred males called drones, whose only function is to fertilize new queens; and up to 60,000 sterile female workers, who do all the work in the hive.

Bee bonnet
Swarms of bees can be very docile. This man probably put the queen in a small cage so that the workers would gather around her.

Lower frame
On the lower frames of a hive (right), honey and pollen are stored in the upper cells, and the brood is reared in the lower cells. When a bee finds a source of nectar, it flies back to the hive and performs a curious "dance" on the comb. This tells other bees how close the food is.

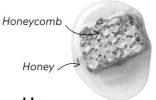

Honeycomb

Honey

Honey
Combs from a hive, with the cells full of honey, are often sold as a delicacy.

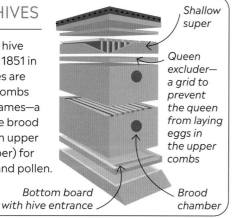

MODERN HIVES

The Langstroth hive was invented in 1851 in the US. The bees are provided with combs in removable frames—a lower set for the brood chamber, and an upper set (shallow super) for storing nectar and pollen.

Shallow super

Queen excluder— a grid to prevent the queen from laying eggs in the upper combs

Bottom board with hive entrance

Brood chamber

Large drone cells

Cell walls are made of wax, which the workers produce in flakes from glands between the joints of their abdomens.

Raina Singhvi Jain

In 2021, American businesswoman Raina Singhvi Jain developed HiveGuard to rid honeybees of *Varroa* mite infections. It is a 3D-printed hive entrance coated with thymol, a nontoxic pesticide. When bees enter the hive, thymol rubs off on their bodies and kills the mites without harming the bees.

Swarming

A bee colony produces a few new queens each year. Just before the first queen emerges from her pupa, the old queen and about half the workers fly away as a swarm. These swarms are usually calm if not provoked and can be transferred to a new home by beekeepers.

White wax-capped cells contain honey for feeding developing grubs.

Yellow-capped cells at top of comb contain pollen stores.

Young C-shaped grubs at bottom of wax cells

Egg

Young grub

Mature grub

Pupa

Life stages

As the eggs develop into grubs, and then pupae, they are fed and looked after by young workers. Older workers look for food outside the hive.

Younger workers keep the cells clean, feed the pupae and grubs, produce wax to build the comb, and guard the hive.

The yellow, silk-capped cells in the lower half of the frame contain larvae and pupae.

Newly hatched grubs are fed first on royal jelly, a special saliva produced by the workers, then on honey.

Helpful and **harmful**

Insects are essential to our well-being. Bees, flies, and butterflies pollinate our crops; wasps and ladybugs destroy the caterpillars and aphids that attack our plants; beetles and flies clean up rotting plants; moth caterpillars produce silk; and food coloring is made from the crushed bodies of certain bugs. However, insects can also be a nuisance. Many insects transmit diseases to people, animals, and plants, and every year they are responsible for the destruction of between 10 and 15 percent of the world's food.

Cochineal insects on a cactus

Dyes

Cochineal is a red food coloring extracted from the crushed bodies of scale insects (*Dactylopius coccus*).

Cochineal coloring

 EYEWITNESS

Leland Ossian Howard
In the 1880s, American entomologist Leland Ossian Howard studied the biological control of insects that carry diseases. In particular, it was his research in medical entomology that identified the common housefly as a major carrier of human diseases, enabling biological control to focus on this species.

Poison darts

The pupae of this African leaf beetle (*Polyclada bohemani*) contain a powerful poison, once used by South African hunters.

Deathwatch beetles

Deathwatch beetles (*Xestobium rufovillosum*) can be serious pests of timber in houses.

Deathwatch beetles can reduce timbers to little more than a skeleton.

Periodic pest

The longhorn beetle (*Hoplocerambyx spinicornis*) usually attacks dead and dying sal trees in India. The grubs drill large tunnels in the timber for feeding and nesting. If the population increases rapidly, it may attack living trees, causing widespread damage.

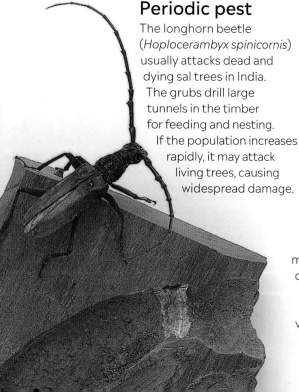

Mining bee collecting nectar and pollen

Hind leg covered with pollen

Little farmers

Pollination is the transfer of pollen grains between the male and female reproductive organs of flowering plants for the purposes of fertilization. Bees and other insects are vital pollinators of crops, fruit trees, and many wild flowers.

Devastating locusts

Most of the time, locusts act like solitary grasshoppers. But when they gather in groups, their body structure, color, and behavior change, and they form swarms. If a swarm breeds uncontrolled for a few months, its numbers can reach thousands of millions. Such a plague will eat all the available plants in an area, leaving the human population destitute.

Adult

Locusts
(*Schistocerca gregaria*)

Nymph

Young nymphs are wingless

Adult locusts have wings

Home wreckers

Termites will sometimes eat away the wooden structure of a house from within the timbers, leaving just the thin painted surface undamaged.

Flour pests

The red-rust flour beetle is a common pest in packets of flour. The larvae of grain weevils live inside the kernels of stored cereals, making them useless for flour production.

Silk moth harvest

Silk has been produced for 5,000 years. Silk moth caterpillars are picked from mulberry trees so that silk can be harvested from their cocoons.

Red-rust flour beetles

Grain weevils

Spider beetles feeding on a dried stock cube

Spider beetles

Both adults and larvae of these spiderlike beetles (*Ptinus tectus*) feed on dried food, spices, and grain. They are common pests in warehouses.

Rolling ball of dung back to nest

Dung beetles

Dung beetles feed on feces and play an important role in preventing it from building up and potentially harming people by becoming a disease risk.

Termites only eat the softer parts of the wood—the hard parts are left.

Looking at **insects**

In the 19th century, interest in natural history became fashionable, and private collections of insects were common. Today, insect collecting is concerned more with examining the ways in which insects help maintain the balance of nature. But looking at insects can be fun. All it requires is patience and good eyesight—possibly helped by a magnifying glass. Just observing how these fascinating creatures live is an important way of learning about the natural world.

Rothamsted Insect Survey

The Rothamsted Insect Survey, UK, is the longest-running insect population study in the world, currently headed by English ecologist James Bell. It started in 1964 and has now collected more than 10 million records, using moth light traps (above) and suction traps to monitor aphids. This has allowed useful estimates of population changes of these insects over that time.

Insect interest

This engraving (left) is of an elaborate glass tank called a vivarium, in which the life cycles of living insects could be observed.

Carrying ring

Chloroform bottle and top

Nozzle

Airtight top

Field diary

The diaries of the English entomologist Charles Dubois (1656-1740) include notes of the insects he saw, often with drawings and comments on their habits and appearance.

Chloroform bottle

Chloroform, kept in containers like this one (right), was once used to kill freshly caught insect specimens.

Finely woven cotton muslin prevents the captured insect from escaping.

Specimen placed in front of lens for examination

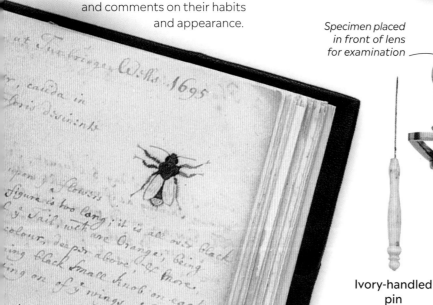

Mounted lens

This mounted lens (left), with its ivory handle, was used for many years by the English collector Edward Meyrick (1854–1938).

Ivory-handled pin

Collecting tin

Insect collectors pinned their fragile specimens in special cork-lined tins like this one (right).

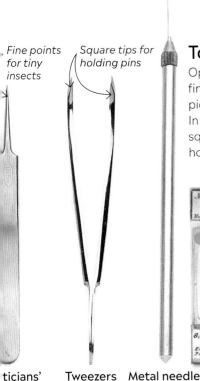

Fine points for tiny insects

Square tips for holding pins

Tools

Opticians' forceps with fine points are useful for picking up tiny specimens. In contrast, tweezers with square tips are used for holding pins.

Labels

The label accompanying a specimen should say where and when the insect was collected and what it was feeding on.

Label

Opticians' forceps   Tweezers   Metal needle holder

Insect pins

Insect pins vary in size. Very small insects are usually stuck onto pieces of card or mounted on microscope slides.

Old pin box

Very fine pins for small insects

Long, stout pins used for larger insects

Microscope slide

Modern plastic collection box

Plastic boxes are lighter than metal ones, and collections can be seen through the lid. Below is a typical collection of small moths.

Scissor net

This old-fashioned scissor net was snapped shut to trap an insect.

Scissorlike handles

Glass dish containing alcohol

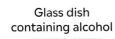

Small insects

Many insect species are too small to be pinned. They are usually collected into alcohol, stored in small glass vials, and studied under a microscope.

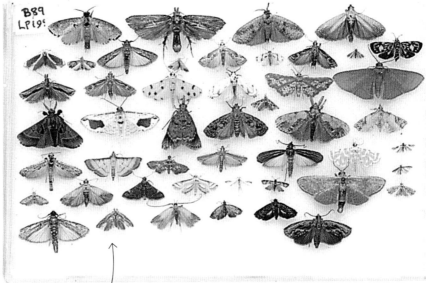

Base of box is lined with white plastic foam

Cork

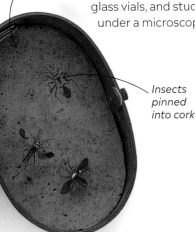

Insects pinned into cork

Moth traps

Moth traps are becoming increasingly popular for studying moths and assessing population changes over time and also for trapping moths to look at and photograph, after which they are released unharmed.

Did you know?

AMAZING FACTS

A cockroach can live for up to three months without its head.

The bombardier beetle defends itself by firing boiling-hot liquid from its abdomen. The gas is formed by a chemical reaction and irritates the eyes of the enemy, acting as a smokescreen while the beetle scuttles off to safety.

The color of an adult head louse can be determined by the color of the person's hair in which it lives.

The tallest known insect nest is one built by a colony of African termites. It measured 42 ft (12.8 m) high.

Queen termites have been known to lay an egg a second—that adds up to an incredible 30 million eggs a year.

One of the most deadly species of insect on Earth is the desert locust, or *Schistocerca gregaria*. It doesn't attack humans or spread disease, but it wreaks havoc on agriculture when a plague of locusts (a swarm) attacks a crop. The desert locust appears after heavy

Young desert locust

Killer bees, or Africanized honeybees

monsoon rains and devours every single plant in an area, often causing famine among local humans and animals.

A swarm of desert locusts may have up to 40 billion members. It can travel 400 sq miles (1,036 sq km) and eat 44,000 tons (40,000 tonnes) of plants a day, enough to feed a city with a population of 400,000 people for a year.

Killer bees, one of the most deadly insects on Earth, are not a naturally occurring species. The bees were first bred in Brazil in 1956, when the African honeybee was crossed with local bees in an attempt to increase their honey yield. However, the

new breed turned out to be aggressive, with a tendency to attack both humans and animals.

Hawk moths can fly at speeds of 33.3 mph (53.6 kph).

The silkworm (*Bombyx mori*) is the caterpillar of a moth whose cocoon is used to make silk. The silk is a single, continuous thread made from protein and secreted by two glands at either side of the caterpillar's head. To harvest, the silkworm is allowed to spin its cocoon and is then placed in boiling water to kill the pupa and help unravel the thread.

Sorting silkworm cocoons to make silk

A man walks safely through a locust swarm

QUESTIONS AND ANSWERS

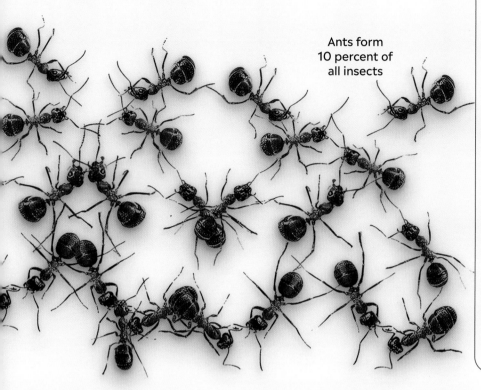

Ants form
10 percent of
all insects

How many species of insects are there overall?

There are at least 1 million different species of insects in total. Insects form around 80 percent of all animal life on Earth and, of this, ants and termites each make up 10 percent. It is estimated that there are 1 billion insects for every human being.

Which insect can withstand the hottest temperatures?

The adults and the larvae of the *Scatella thermarum* fly are found in hot springs in Iceland and can live in temperatures as hot as 118°F (48°C), which is too hot for most people to put their hands into.

What is the best way to repel insects?

Natural insect repellents that can be worn on the skin include oil mixtures containing cedar, tea tree, lavender, or vanilla. Some people believe that eating garlic may keep insects at bay—especially blood-hungry pests such as mosquitoes. This is because garlic emits an odor when absorbed into the blood, which many insects find unpleasant.

What is an insect's favorite food?

Although many insects have very precise diets, some are not fussy and will eat almost anything, including wood, shoe polish, and paper!

Can insects be eaten?

Many peoples of the world include insects as part of a nutritious diet. One example is the annual moth feast held by the Aboriginal peoples in the Bogong mountains of New South Wales, Australia. Moths are cooked in hot sand. After the heads have been removed, the moths' bodies are ground into a paste and baked as cakes. Other popular insect meals around the world include fried grasshoppers, roasted crickets, and larvae paste.

Do insects have brains?

Yes. An ant brain, for example, has about 250,000 brain cells. A human brain has 10,000 million cells, so a colony of 40,000 ants has collectively the same-size brain power as a human being.

Garlic can keep
insects at bay

What is the biggest ant colony ever known?

A supercolony of *Formica yessensis* on the coast of Japan is reported to have been home to more than 1 million queens and 306 million worker ants living in 45,000 interlinked nests underground.

Which insect has the longest body?

One species of stick insect, *Pharnacia kirbyi*, has the longest body of all insects. Females can reach up to 14 in (36 cm) long.

Which is the loudest insect?

The African cicada *Brevisana brevis* produces a sound pressure at a level of 106.7 decibels over a distance of 19.5 in (50 cm). This is the loudest insect call on record. Insect songs form a vital part of communication, defense, and reproduction.

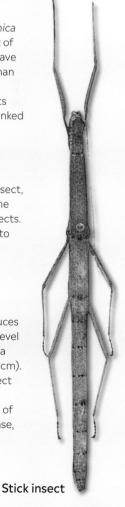

Stick insect

Insect classification

There are more than 1 million species of known insects in the world. Here are the main insect groups.

Flies, gnats, and mosquitoes

Including around 90,000 species, this group contains the household fly as well as bloodsuckers such as mosquitoes. Flies can transmit diseases by contaminating food with organisms picked up on their legs and mouthparts.

The hover fly is often mistaken for a wasp.

Hover fly

Flying cockroach

Cockroaches

Cockroaches include around 5,500 different species and have been present on Earth for more than 400 million years. Cockroaches are very sturdy insects and can run at speeds of nearly 1.8 mph (3 kph).

Buff-tailed bumblebee

Bugs

This group includes greenflies, shield bugs, cicadas, and water striders. Shield bugs are often called "stink bugs" because they can produce a horrible smell by emitting a fluid from their glands.

Shield bug

Crab louse

Bees and wasps

Although feared for their stings, bees and wasps are key to flower pollination and feed on smaller insects that are harmful to crops. They are social creatures that often live in communities.

Lice

These wingless parasites infest humans and animals, laying eggs in hair-covered parts of the body and feeding on skin and blood.

Stick insects

Containing around 2,500 species, these insects are mostly found in the tropics. Stick insects may or may not have wings and are often bred as pets.

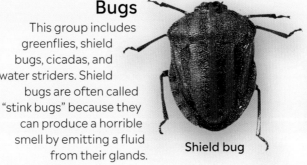

Stick insect

Eyespots may divert predators away from delicate body.

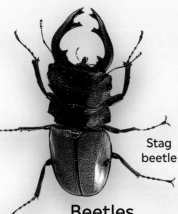

Stag beetle

Ant

Swallowtail butterfly

Beetles

The largest single group in insect classification, beetles include animals as diverse as the wingless glowworm, the woodworm, and the ladybug.

Ants

Ants are among the most numerous of the insect species and make up around 10 percent of all animal life on Earth.

Butterflies and moths

Numbering more than 300,000 species in all, this group can be found all over the world.

Stone flies

So called because they are often seen resting on stones, these aquatic insects number around 2,000 named species. They are a favorite food of fish such as trout.

Praying mantises

There are about 1,700 varieties of praying mantis. Most species live in warm climates. The female mantis may eat the male after mating.

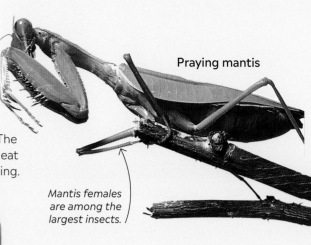

Praying mantis

Mantis females are among the largest insects.

Scorpionfly

Silverfish

Fleas

Flea

Feeding off animals, a flea's diet consists of blood. An average flea can consume up to 15 times its own body weight in blood daily. This insect spends 95 percent of its life as an egg, larva, or pupa and only 5 percent as an adult. Adult fleas cannot survive without regular blood meals.

Scorpionflies

This small group includes only 400 species, most of which measure around 0.8 in (2 cm) in length. They get their name from the male tail, which is turned upward like a scorpion's, although it carries no sting.

Bristletails

The 600 species of bristletails are found worldwide. Silverfish do not have any wings and are often found scavenging for food in domestic households.

Dragonflies

Dragonflies are so called because of their fierce jaws, although they actually use their legs to catch prey. These insects were in existence long before the dinosaurs.

Grasshopper

Thrips love to feed on flowers.

Grasshoppers and crickets

This group contains 17,000 species and also includes the voracious desert locust. Crickets have long antennae, and many species are called "katydids" in North America.

Dragonfly

Thrips

These tiny insects measure just 0.1 in (0.25 cm) in length and number around 3,000 species. They live among crops and can cause real damage to harvests.

Mayflies

These beautiful insects can spend up to three years as a nymph and then perish after just a few hours as an adult.

Lacewings

So called because of their delicate, veined wings, this insect group includes more than 6,000 species. Lacewing larvae hide from their predators under the empty skins of their prey.

Lacewing

Lacewings feed on other insects.

Adult mayflies cannot eat, so they die quickly.

Mayfly

Find out more

To get more insight into the world of creepy crawlies without getting too up close and personal, check out your nearest natural history museum. Here, you can examine preserved insect specimens kept safely at bay behind glass! However, some of the most fun expeditions can start at home.

Natural history museum
One of the best places to learn about insects is at a natural history museum, such as the Natural History Museum, London, UK (above). Here, you can find exhibitions of ancient and modern insects, carefully collected through the years.

Natural history exhibitions
When you visit a natural history museum, there will usually be a section devoted to entomology. Here, you can view preserved specimens of many exotic species from around the globe.

USEFUL WEBSITES

- Search for an insect on this comprehensive database
  www.whatsthatbug.com

- Buglife: an illustrated database of a variety of bugs
  www.buglife.org.uk/bugs/identify-a-bug

- Website of London's Natural History Museum, featuring the museum's vast insect collection
  www.nhm.ac.uk/our-science/collections/entomology-collections.html

Countryside
On your field trip, look closely at the ground and you will find busy colonies working away. In summer, you can also observe insects in search of nectar on clusters of flowers.

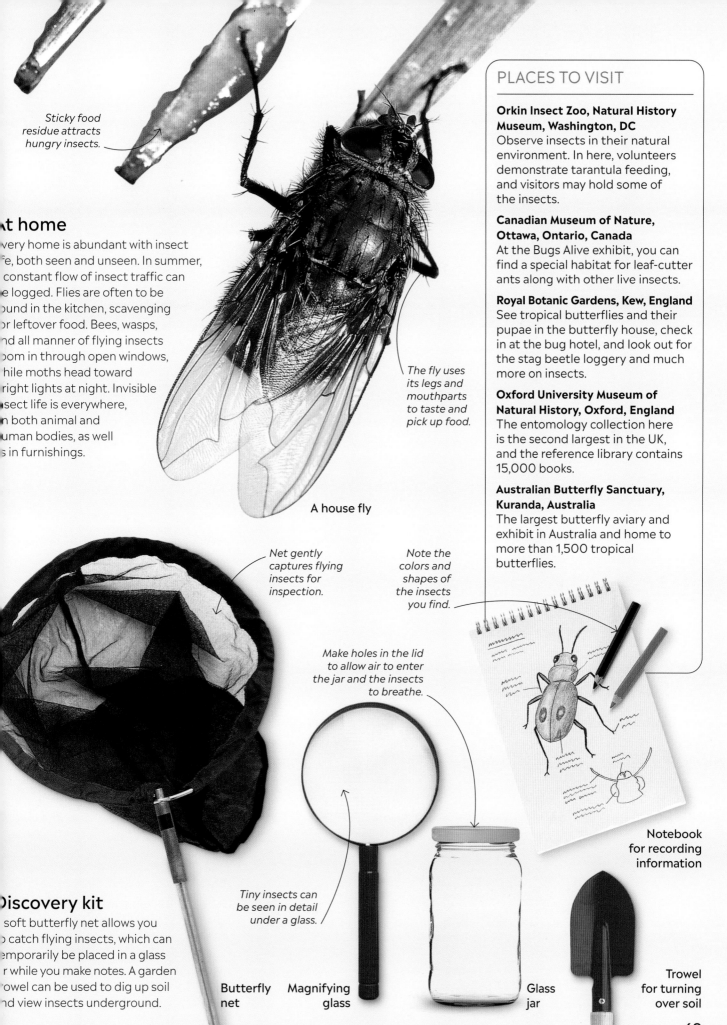

Sticky food residue attracts hungry insects.

...t home

...very home is abundant with insect ...fe, both seen and unseen. In summer, ...constant flow of insect traffic can ...e logged. Flies are often to be ...ound in the kitchen, scavenging ...or leftover food. Bees, wasps, ...nd all manner of flying insects ...oom in through open windows, ...hile moths head toward ...right lights at night. Invisible ...sect life is everywhere, ...n both animal and ...uman bodies, as well ...s in furnishings.

The fly uses its legs and mouthparts to taste and pick up food.

A house fly

PLACES TO VISIT

Orkin Insect Zoo, Natural History Museum, Washington, DC
Observe insects in their natural environment. In here, volunteers demonstrate tarantula feeding, and visitors may hold some of the insects.

Canadian Museum of Nature, Ottawa, Ontario, Canada
At the Bugs Alive exhibit, you can find a special habitat for leaf-cutter ants along with other live insects.

Royal Botanic Gardens, Kew, England
See tropical butterflies and their pupae in the butterfly house, check in at the bug hotel, and look out for the stag beetle loggery and much more on insects.

Oxford University Museum of Natural History, Oxford, England
The entomology collection here is the second largest in the UK, and the reference library contains 15,000 books.

Australian Butterfly Sanctuary, Kuranda, Australia
The largest butterfly aviary and exhibit in Australia and home to more than 1,500 tropical butterflies.

Net gently captures flying insects for inspection.

Note the colors and shapes of the insects you find.

Make holes in the lid to allow air to enter the jar and the insects to breathe.

Notebook for recording information

...iscovery kit

... soft butterfly net allows you ...o catch flying insects, which can ...emporarily be placed in a glass ...r while you make notes. A garden ...rowel can be used to dig up soil ...nd view insects underground.

Tiny insects can be seen in detail under a glass.

Butterfly net

Magnifying glass

Glass jar

Trowel for turning over soil

Glossary

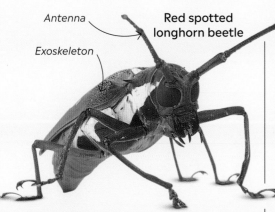

Antenna
Exoskeleton
Red spotted
longhorn beetle

ABDOMEN
The rear part of an insect's body.

ANTENNAE
The sensory organs on each side of the head, also called feelers, used for navigation, taste, "sight," and hearing.

ARTHROPOD
An invertebrate with a jointed body case, such as an insect or a spider. Insects and spiders are often confused with each other, but unlike spiders, insects have three separate body parts, three pairs of legs, and antennae.

BENEFICIAL INSECTS
Any insect that has a lifestyle that is beneficial to humans, such as pollinators and recyclers.

CAMOUFLAGE
When an insect adopts the color or texture of its surrounding environment to conceal itself from predators or prey.

CATERPILLAR
The larva of a moth, butterfly, or sawfly.

CERCI
The paired structures that spring from the tip of the abdomen in many insects.

CHITIN
The tough material that makes up an insect's exoskeleton.

CHRYSALIS
The pupa of a butterfly or moth.

COCOON
A covering composed either partly or wholly of silk and spun by many larvae as a protection for the pupae.

COLONY
A local population, often produced by a single queen.

COMPOUND EYE
An eye made up of hundreds of mini-eyes called ommatidia or facets.

ENTOMOLOGY
The study of insects. An entomologist is a scientist who studies insects.

ENVELOPE
A protective covering made by some wasps for their nests. In common wasps, the envelope is constructed from chewed wood fibers and saliva.

EXOSKELETON
The hard outer case that surrounds an insect's body.

GRUB
A thick-bodied larva with thoracic legs (legs attached to the thorax) and a well developed head.

HIND
Relating to the back part, such as hind legs or hind wings.

INVERTEBRATE
An animal without a backbone.

LARVA
An immature insect that looks different from its parents and often eats different food. When a larva is mature, it undergoes complete metamorphosis.

MAGGOT
A larva without legs and without a well-developed head.

MANDIBLES
The first pair of jaws in insects. These are toothlike in chewing insects, pointed in sucking insects, and form the upper jaw of biting insects.

MAXILLA
The second pair of jaws that some insects possess.

METAMORPHOSIS
The series of changes that an insect undergoes between its early life and adulthood. Insects that undergo incomplete metamorphosis change gradually as they grow up. Ones that undergo complete metamorphosis change abruptly during a resting stage called a pupa.

MOLTING
In insects, the process of shedding the exoskeleton.

MOTTLED
A surface with blotchy color variation or difference.

NECTAR
The sugary liquid secreted by many flowers on which some insects feed.

Centipede, an arthropod but not an insect

NYMPH
The name given to the young stages of insect that undergo incomplete metamorphosis. The nymph is usually similar to the adult except that its wings are not fully developed.

OCELLUS
The simple eyes in larvae, which detect light and dark but cannot form images.

OOTHECA
An egg case, such as the purselike structure carried around by cockroaches

OVIPOSITOR
The tubular egg-laying apparatus of a female insect.

PALP
A segmented leglike structure. Palps have a sensory function and play a role in tasting food.

Crow
swallowtail
caterpillar

Antenna

Butterflies undergo metamorphosis

PARASITE
An organism that spends part or all of its life in close association with another species, taking food from it but giving nothing in return.

POLLEN
Fertilizing powder or grains produced by a flower and often carried from plant to plant by insects.

PREDATOR
An insect that preys on or hunts another animal to kill it for food.

PROBOSCIS
Any extended mouth structure, usually applied to the mouth of flies, the beak of bugs, and the tongue of butterflies and moths.

PROLEG
An insect larva's abdominal leg, distinguished from a "true" leg.

PUPA
The stage of complete metamorphosis between larva and adult.

QUEEN CELL
The cell in which a queen honeybee develops from egg to adult.

ROSTRUM
A snout or beaklike feature; usually refers to a piercing mouthpart.

SCAVENGER
An insect that feeds on human waste or on dead plants or animals.

SEGMENT
One of the rings or divisions of the body, or one of the sections of a jointed limb.

SOCIAL INSECTS
Insects such as ants or bees that live in organized communities of individuals.

SOLDIER
In termites and ants, soldiers protect and guard the colony from intruders and predators.

TARSUS
The foot or jointed appendage at the end of the leg.

TIBIA
The fourth joint of an insect's leg.

THORAX
The second or intermediate part of the body, corresponding roughly to the chest region in humans.

TRACHEAE
Tubes in the body that transport oxygen.

TRUE FLIES
Those flies that have only one pair of wings. The remnants of a second pair of wings, known as halteres, function as stabilizers or airspeed detectors during flight.

TYMPANUM
The vibratory membrane in various parts of an insect's body that serves as an eardrum.

ULTRAVIOLET
Beyond the violet end of the light spectrum, ultraviolet is invisible to most mammals but visible to most insects.

WORKER
A member of an insect colony that is sterile (cannot breed) and whose duties include finding food for the colony.

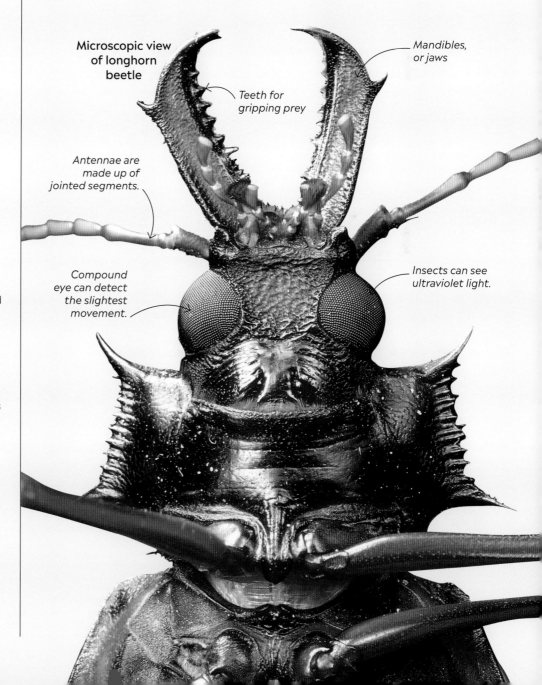

Microscopic view of longhorn beetle

Mandibles, or jaws

Teeth for gripping prey

Antennae are made up of jointed segments.

Compound eye can detect the slightest movement.

Insects can see ultraviolet light.

Index

Acknowledgments

The author would like to thank his many colleagues at the Natural History Museum who helped with this project, particularly Sharon Shute, Judith Marshall, Bill Dolling, George Else, David Carter, Nigel Fergusson, John Chainey, Steve Brooks, Nigel Wyatt, Philip Ackery, Peter Broomfield, Bill Sands, Barry Bolton, Mick Day, and Dick Vane-Wright.

Dorling Kindersley would like to thank:
Julie Harvey at the Natural History Museum; London Zoo; Dave King for special photography on pp.56-57; David Burnie and Dr. George McGavin for consultancy; Kathy Lockley for picture research; Claire Bowers, David Ekholm-JAlbum, Sunita Gahir, Jo Little, Nigel Ritchie, Susan St. Louis, Carey Scott, and Bulent Yusuf for the clipart; David Ball, Neville Graham, Rose Horridge, Jo Little, and Sue Nicholson for the wallchart; BCP, Marianne Petrou, and Owen Peyton Jones for checking the digitized files; and Hazel Beynon for editing the relaunch version and Victoria Pyke for proofreading it.

For this edition, the publisher would also like to thank:
Camilla Hallinan and Anita Kakar for editorial assistance; Anastasia Baliyan for design assistance; Scarlett O'Hara for proofreading; and Elizabeth Wise for indexing.

The publisher would like to thank the following for their kind permission to reproduce their images:

Picture credits

b = bottom, c = center, f = far,
l = left, m = middle, r = right, t = top
Alamy Stock Photo: J. M. Barres / Agefotostock 36bc, Marc Anderson 57tr, Dpa picture alliance archive 42cl, World History Archive 60tr, Gordon Bell 69tr, Blickwinkel / H. Bellmann 31bc,

Michel Gunther / Biosphoto 35cla, 99Wallchartcb, Veronica Carte 42cra, Thomas Cockrem 52bc, The History Collection 35tc, IanDagnall Computing 25tr, Dom Greves 33bl, David Havel 34bl, Robert Hoetink 19bl, Justus de Cuveland / ImageBROKER 47tr, John Insull 29tr, Intellifix 34cb, Andy lane 68cl, Frans lemmens 59tr, Liquid Light 36tr, Jose ramon polo lopez 61bl, PAUL R. STERRY / Nature Photographers Ltd. 63br, BJ Warnick / Newscom 56tr, Gary Parker 15br, Edward Phillips 21ca, Nature Photographers Ltd. 3cla, Nature Photographers Ltd. 34tr, Ingo Arndt / Minden Pictures 46bl, Minden Pictures 12tr, Stephen Dalton / Minden Pictures 37cla, Morley Read 57ca, BAZ RATNER / Reuters 41cr, Scenics & Science 36cl, Shotshop GmbH 11tr, Richard Smith 41cra, Blickwinkel / R. Sturm 20tr, Urbach, James / SuperStock 34tr (Long-tailed skipper), Survivalphotos 21bl, Tom Tookey 4br, 41tc, Malcolm Walker 62tr, Wirestock, Inc. 9cra, Peter Yeeles 57tc; **Aldus Archive:** 61clb. **Angel, Heather/ Biophotos:** 10cb; **Biophoto Associates:** 36cr; 41bc. **Borrch, B./Frank Lane:** 18tl. **Borrell, B./Frank Lane:** 56tr, 67cr. **Bunn, D. S.:** 50tr **Burton, Jane/Bruce Coleman:** 31b; 39ca. **Cane, W./Natural Science Photos:** 32m; 61bm. **Clarke, Dave:** 23tr 47b. **Corbis:** Benjamin Lowy 68bl. **Couch, Carolyn/ Natural History Museum:** 15br. **Craven, Philip/ Robert Harding Picture Library:** 7t. **Dalton, Stephen/NHPA:** 37ml. **Courtesy of FAAM:** BAE Systems Regional Aircraft 12-13ca; With thanks to Maureen Smith and the Met Office UK. Photo by Doug Anderson 13cr. **Dreamstime.com:** Alexander Hasenkampf 39tl, Jmrocek 22-23c, 99Wallchartcra, Klomsky 42c, Mbridger68 23tr, Martin Pelanek 30cr, Pimmimemom 34cl, Manfred Ruckszio 34cl (Swallowtail pupa), Saknakorn 18-19cb (Background), 28-29b, S. Walker 36br; **Foto Natura Stock/FLPA:** 66cr. **George, Poinar:** 10c; **Goodman, Jeff/NHPA:** 9ml. **Hellio & Van Ingen/NHPA:** 64bl; **Getty Images:** Mark Evers—500px 15tc, Sirisak Boakaew 69b, Antony Cooper 15cra, Paul Starosta / Stone 44l, Westend61 14-15c; **Getty Images/iStock:** Henrik_L 7br, Macbrianmun 42tr,

Luc Pouliot 40bc, SanderMeertins 40br, Court Whelan 35r; **Holford, Michael:** 15mr. **Kate Umbers:** Nola Umbers 47br; **Krist, Bob/Corbis:** 68cr. **Lofthouse, Barbara:** 25tc. **Mackenzie, M. A./Robert Harding Picture Library:** 37br. **Mary Evans Picture Library:** 61ca, 64cr. **Minden Pictures/FLPA:** 71b. **Natural History Museum:** 12cr, 14bl, 65tr, 66c. **naturepl. com:** Sue Daly 22cl, Mitsuaki Iwago 57tl; **Nikki Gammans:** Bumblebee Conservation Trust 38cra. **Norina Vicente:** Piotr Naskrecki 51tr; **Oliver, Stephen:** 69bc. **Packwood, Richard/ Oxford scientific Films:** 56tr. **Polking, Fritz/FLPA:** 64tl. **Popperphoto:** 61tl. **Raina Singhvi Jain:** 59tc; **Rutherford, Gary/Bruce Coleman:** 7bm. **Sands, Bill:** 55m. **Science Photo Library:** World History Archive 61br, Steve Gschmeissner 39tr, AMI Images 16bl, Ingo Arndt/ Nature Picture Library 61tl, Mark Bowler / Nature Picture Library 47tl, David Scharf 15crb; **Shaw, John/Bruce Coleman Ltd.:** 67br. **Shutterstock.com:** Alslutsky 3cra, Wirestock Creators 38c, Danielkreissl 99Wallchartcb (Euplagia quadripunctaria), Rhonny dayusasono 67bl, Gstalker 39tc, Henrik Larsson 67br, Andrey Pavlov 39br, Marek R. Swadzba 32tr, Wesleylilin 33br; **Tarun Karmakar:** 36clb; **Taylor, Kim/ Bruce Coleman:** 21tl; 31b. **Taylor, Kim:** 33m. **Williams, C./ Natural Science Photos:** 36cr. **Wellcome Collection:** 60cl **Young, Jerry:** 66bl.

Illustrations: John Woodcock: 10, 41, 55; Nick Hall: 13, 15 **Wallchart: Alamy Images:** Michael Freeman br; **BAE Systems Regional Aircraft:** fcl (Aircraft); **Corbis:** crb; Lynsey Addario bl; Roger Ressmeyer cr (Lightning); **FAAM/Doug Anderson, Maureen Smith & Met office UK:** cl; **Science Photo Library:** NOAA cl (Storm)
All other images © Dorling Kindersley

For further information, see:
www.dkimages.com